EZEKIEL: THE MAN AND HIS MESSAGE

EZEKIEL:

THE MAN AND HIS MESSAGE

By

H. L. ELLISON, B.A., B.D.

"It was Ezekiel who saw the vision of glory,
Which God shewed him upon the chariot of the cherubim."

(Ben Sira 49: 8.)

Wm. B. Eerdmans Publishing Company
Grand Rapids, Michigan

PHOTOLITHOPRINTED BY CUSHING - MALLOY, INC.
ANN ARBOR, MICHIGAN, UNITED STATES OF AMERICA

To

THE DESIRE OF MY EYES

who is yet with me

(24: 16)

CONTENTS

CHAP.   PAGE

LIST OF ABBREVIATIONS – – – – – 9

INTRODUCTION – – – – – – – 11

THE STRUCTURE OF EZEKIEL – – – – 13

CHRONOLOGICAL OUTLINE – – – – – 13

I THE MAN AND HIS TIMES – – – – – 15
(Ch. 1: 1–3)

II THE VISION OF GOD – – – – – – 22
(Ch. 1:4–2:2)

III GOD'S SERVANT – – – – – – – 27
(Ch. 2:3–3:21)

IV THE FIRST PROPHECIES – – – – – 31
(Ch. 3:22–7:27)

V ICHABOD – – – – – – – – 40
(Ch. 8:1–11:25)

VI WOE TO THE PROPHETS – – – – – 50
(Ch. 12:1–15:8)

VII JERUSALEM, QUEEN AND HARLOT – – – 61
(Ch. 16:1–17:24)

VIII GOD AND THE INDIVIDUAL – – – – – 71
(Ch. 18:1–19:14)

IX THE FAILURE OF ISRAEL – – – – – 77
(Ch. 20: 1–44)

X THE BLOODY CITY – – – – – – 84
(Ch. 20:45–23:49)

XI THE MIDNIGHT HOUR – – – – – 96
(Ch. 24: 1–27)

8 CONTENTS

CHAP.

PAGE

XII THE PROPHECIES AGAINST THE NATIONS – – 99
(Ch. 25:1–32:32)

XIII PROPHECIES OF RESTORATION – – – – 117
(Ch. 33:1–39:29)

XIV THE LORD IS THERE – – – – – – 137
(Ch. 40:1–48:35)

LIST OF ABBREVIATIONS

This work uses standard abbreviations for the names of the books of the Bible as well as many in common use. Only the following need mention.

a (b, c, d)	refers to the first (second, third or fourth) part of the verse mentioned.
ad loc.	at the appropriate place.
AJV	The American Jewish Version of 1917.
Aquila	A 2nd cent. A.D. translation of O.T. into Greek.
Cam.B.	Cambridge Bible for Schools and Colleges; the volume on Ezekiel is by Davidson and Streane.
f.	and the following verse, or chapter.
ff.	and the following two verses, or chapters.
ICC	International Critical Commentary; the volume on Ezekiel is by G. A. Cooke.
Knox	Translation by Monsignor Knox; O.T. in 1949.
LXX	Septuagint, the standard Greek translation of O.T.; Ezekiel about 150 B.C.
mg.	margin.
Moffatt	Translation by James Moffatt; O.T. in 1924.
NBC	*The New Bible Commentary* (1953).
RSV	Revised Standard Version; O.T. in 1952.
RV	Revised Version; O.T. in 1885.
Syriac	or Peshitta, an East Aramaic translation going back to the 2nd cent. A.D.
Targum	The official Aramaic translation (sometimes paraphrases) of the O.T.; the Targum on Ezekiel may in essence be as old as 1st cent. A.D.
Theodotion	A 2nd cent. A.D. translation of O.T. into Greek, somewhat later than Aquila.
tx.	Text.
Vulgate	The Latin translation of the Bible made by Jerome between A.D. 382 and 405.

INTRODUCTION

THOUGH a number of works on Ezekiel intended for the scholar have appeared in recent years, there is very little for the serious student of Scripture who is not concerned with critical problems and who is unable to read the prophet in the original.

This study has taken into consideration the rush of modern life, which makes it difficult for so many to give long hours of study to an individual Old Testament book; it has also borne in mind that those who will probably welcome it most are just those who can least afford expensive works. I have tried to make Ezekiel's message clear by taking his prophecy chapter by chapter and section by section. Though I have not consciously glossed over any difficulty in the book, I have ignored all critical questions which I considered to have no direct bearing on the interpretation, and where the text of the Revised Version seemed to make the sense tolerably clear, I have refrained from pedantic exactitude. Where the meaning of the message has seemed obvious, I have not hesitated to dismiss a chapter in a paragraph. The space so saved has been used for fuller discussion of problems which either have contemporary interest, or are generally misunderstood by the average Bible student.

Those who regard the prophets mainly as guides to the future are likely to be disappointed by this work. For me "the prophet speaks *primarily* to the men of his own time, and his message springs out of the circumstances in which he lives."[1] Hence we will best understand Ezekiel as we try to grasp what his own generation should have understood and only then reinterpret, if necessary, in the light of the New Testament. In dealing with the prophecies of the future I have therefore been normally more concerned with what Ezekiel's contemporaries were to understand by them than with what we may read into them from the standpoint of the New Testament. Where eschatology enters a work of this kind, it is necessary to make certain assumptions unless one has unlimited space for digressions. I have assumed that after the Second Advent of Christ there will be a long period in which God's original purpose in creating nature around us will be displayed and vindicated; in

[1] My *Men Spake from God*, p. 14.

11

this period the nations that have only imperfectly been embraced in the Church's missionary work will have the knowledge of God brought to them. I have applied the term Millennium to this period, but I must not be taken to be saying Amen to much of the gross materialism that is postulated of this period in so much popular literature. For me the Millennium is essentially the time in which the limitations of the earthly are prepared for the eternal state; my thinking on this subject has been deeply influenced by P. Althaus: *Die Letzten Dinge*.

This work is intended not to give my views on Ezekiel, but to help Ezekiel speak to the present age. Hence the reader will lose much of its value unless the Revised Version is open before him as well. If he uses the Authorized or King James' Version, he is apt to meet only vexation in some of the more difficult passages. Normally I have made no reference to the incorrect renderings of AV.

I owe a deep debt to Dr. G. A. Cooke's commentary on *Ezekiel* in the International Critical Commentary and to a less extent to the corresponding volume in the Cambridge Bible for Schools and Colleges for their help in the many difficult passages, where the language is hard to interpret. The ordinary reader failing to find some linguistic point adequately dealt with here cannot do better than refer to the latter volume. The interpretation of the thought is, however, mine alone, for I have not hesitated to follow what seemed to me to be the guidance of the Holy Spirit; let His be the praise and mine the blame. Periodically I have disagreed with those whose views I respect; in these cases I have normally referred in a footnote to some treatment of the subject that presents the other side.

Those familiar with my *Men Spake from God* will notice that in a number of points I have changed my opinion. That is how it should be. One cannot live with a man like Ezekiel for nearly four years—most of this work has appeared first in quarterly instalments in that estimable but all too little known periodical *The Bible Student*—without his growing immeasurably in stature and as a result some of one's views, especially the more critical, changing.

I have deliberately omitted an index partly to keep the price of the book down, partly because it seemed unnecessary. Since the order of Ezekiel is preserved and there are many subheadings and cross-references, it should be possible to find the treatment of any desired point at least as quickly as if there were an index.

H. L. ELLISON.

THE STRUCTURE OF EZEKIEL

A. Ch. 1–3: 21   Ezekiel's Call
   1. Ch. 1   The Vision of God
   2. Ch. 2–3: 21   The Prophet's Commissioning

B. Ch. 3: 22–24: 27   Prophecies of Doom
   1. Ch. 3: 22–7: 27   The Opening Messages of Judgment
   2. Ch. 8–19   The Sin of Jerusalem
   3. Ch. 20–23   The Foulness of Jerusalem's Sin
   4. Ch. 24   The Midnight Hour

C. Ch. 25–32   Prophecies against the Nations
   1. Ch. 25   Judah's Neighbours
   2. Ch. 26–28   Tyre
   3. Ch. 29–32   Egypt

D. Ch. 33–39   Prophecies of Restoration
   1. Ch. 33   The Prophet's Function
   2. Ch. 34   Rulers Past and Future
   3. Ch. 35   The Enemies of Israel
   4. Ch. 36   The New Covenant
   5. Ch. 37   National Resurrection
   6. Ch. 38, 39   The Last Enemies

E. Ch. 40–48   The People of God
   1. Ch. 40–43   The Temple
   2. Ch. 44–46   The Worship
   3. Ch. 47: 1–12   The River
   4. Ch. 47:13–48:35   The Land and the City

CHRONOLOGICAL OUTLINE

609 B.C.   Battle of Megiddo; death of Josiah

605   Battle of Carchemish; Babylon supreme

597   Jehoiachin deported to Babylon

592   Ezekiel's call

588   Zedekiah's revolt

586   The fall of Jerusalem

571   Last dated prophecy of Ezekiel (29: 17–20)

562   Death of Nebuchadnezzar

560   Release of Jehoiachin (II Kings 25: 27–30)

538   Capture of Babylon by Cyrus

CHAPTER I

THE MAN AND HIS TIMES

E ZEKIEL—for some the framer of choice problems, whether it be the chariot-throne of God, the *merkabah*, or the blueprints of a temple yet to be; for others a foreteller hard to interpret; for yet others the giver of a few of the choicest promises in the Old Testament; for the vast majority an enigma, with the bulk of his writings unstudied and unappreciated. There are two adequate reasons for this.

First there is the man himself. In any society and at any time he would have been regarded as abnormal. Then he is bound to the circumstances of his own time as virtually no other prophet. He is the only prophet—apart from Haggai and Zechariah (ch. 1–8), who may well have been influenced by him —who carefully dates *all* the sections of his prophecy. This is not just because Ezekiel had a tidy mind, but because his prophecies cannot be fully understood without a knowledge of their historical background. The same is true of Haggai and Zechariah, ch. 1–8. It will be found elsewhere in the prophets that a date is normally an invitation to the prior study of the historical circumstances out of which the prophecy came. I am suggesting not that a prophecy cannot be understood without such a study, but that it cannot be *fully* understood.

THE HISTORICAL BACKGROUND

When Josiah came to the throne in 639 B.C., Judah was firmly in the grip of Assyria, but already as Ashurbanipal's long reign drew to its close a new hope of freedom began to blossom. With his death (633 B.C.) Assyria's power rapidly crumbled. Josiah's reformation, which reached its height in 621 B.C., was as much political as religious, an outward sign of the throwing off of the Assyrian yoke. Josiah was able to extend his power through Mount Ephraim and the Plain of Esdraelon into Eastern Galilee (II Chron. 34: 6). Jeremiah saw early that the reformation was spiritually a failure—see Jer. 5, a chapter that on internal evidence must be dated soon after 621 B.C. The collapse of the enlarged kingdom after Josiah's death at Megiddo in 609 B.C. (II Kings 23: 29f.) showed that the political dreams were equally vain. For a time Jehoiakim was a vassal of Egypt, but after Nebuchadnezzar's great victory over Pharaoh Necho at Carchemish in 605 B.C. all the lands down to the frontier of Egypt submitted at once to him.

Jehoiakim, in spite of his insignificance, dreamt his dreams of greatness (Jer. 22: 13–19; the building of a new palace was symbolic of a new beginning); he willingly lent his ear to the suggestions of Egypt and rebelled (II Kings 24: 1). He met an obscure and ignoble end, and Jehoiachin, his son, made haste to surrender (II Kings 24: 8–12) as soon as Nebuchadnezzar had invested Jerusalem (597 B.C.). The Babylonian king decided that drastic steps were needed. He never formally deposed Jehoiachin—we gather this from official ration documents discovered on the site of Babylon; note also that Ezekiel dates by the years of Jehoiachin's captivity (1: 2, etc.) and see II Kings 25: 27–30—but took him away to Babylon, leaving his uncle Zedekiah to rule as a sort of king-regent in his place. With him he took most of the influential people (II Kings 24: 14). The intention was to leave the people virtually leaderless looking to Babylon, where their rightful king was, but he had not allowed for Zedekiah's weakness or the fanaticism of many of those who remained in Jerusalem.

At first a spirit of optimism will have prevailed among many of the captives. Hananiah was prophesying in Jerusalem that they would return with the temple vessels in two years' time (Jer. 28). In Babylonia itself there were "prophets" among the captives who, though perhaps not so precise, were foretelling a speedy return (Jer. 29: 8). Jeremiah's letter (Jer. 29), and the death of Hananiah (Jer. 28: 15–17), and of Ahab and Zedekiah (Jer. 29: 21–23), as prophesied by Jeremiah, destroyed any hopes of a speedy return.

EZEKIEL'S BACKGROUND

Ezekiel came of a priestly family (1: 3). We know nothing of his father Buzi, but we have every reason for thinking that he belonged to the more influential circles of the priesthood. This is suggested partly by the respect shown to Ezekiel by the elders of the people in exile (8:1; 14:1; 20:1), but even more by the fact that Ezekiel, though young, was included among the captives.

The dating in Ezekiel is throughout in the years of Jehoiachin's captivity, i.e. beginning from 597 B.C., except the mention of the 30th year in 1:1. Every type of explanation for this date has been attempted, but the only one that would seem to hold water is that it means Ezekiel's 30th year. Jewish tradition is of no help here; the suggestion that it refers to Ezekiel's age seems to have been first made by the Church-Father Origen (†253). Many of the suggestions by modern scholars assume a corruption of the text.

Strangely enough neither in the Old Testament nor in the traditions of the Jews as preserved in the Talmud and other Rabbinic writings have we any indication of the age at which a priest began his service. This may be due to the necessity of exceptionally early service, if the high priest, or some other in special office, died comparatively young. Note in this connexion that as no descendants of Nadab and Abihu are ever mentioned, it may be that they were quite young at the time of their sudden death (Lev. 10: 1, 2). There is, however, an intrinsic probability that the normal age for entering on priestly service was thirty as with the Levites (Num. 4: 3).[1] This may be the explanation of the age of our Lord at His baptism.

If this is correct, Ezekiel will never have functioned as priest in the temple at Jerusalem. It was, however, expected of the priest that he should be meticulously accurate in every detail of the traditional ritual, so a long period of preparation was necessary for the young men of priestly family. No very close reading of his writings is called for to show us that Ezekiel was steeped in the traditions of the priesthood. If he was a young man of twenty-five when he was taken off by Nebuchadnezzar in 597 B.C., he may well have been preparing for his anticipated life-work for at least five years before. For few of the captives can deportation have been a greater blow, for it seemed to mean the end of all real purpose in life.

It should be easy to picture his distress as his thirtieth birthday drew near, and he thought of the temple far to the west, where, if Jeremiah's words were true, he would never have the privilege of serving.

EZEKIEL AND SYMBOLISM

It is necessary to stress Ezekiel's priestly background and training, for they explain that element in his prophecies that the modern Christian finds hardest to understand, an element that may even repel him.

Symbolism is familiar to Christians from the Tabernacle and its sacrifices, and from the Christian sacraments. In its religious sense symbolism means that a building, a dress, action,

[1] This is not the place to deal with the apparent discrepancies between Num. 4: 3; Num. 8: 24 and I Chron. 23: 24. I Chron. 23: 3 shows that the law of Num. 4: 3 was still in force in David's time, nor could he have changed it. The younger ages were probably for initiatory and more menial service.

form of words, or whatever is involved have a deeper spiritual meaning than a merely literal interpretation would suggest. If that meaning is prophetic of our Lord, we normally speak of a type rather than a symbol.

Since a spiritual truth is never completely expressible in words, symbolism probably plays some part, consciously or unconsciously, in the life of every Christian. On the whole, however, in modern urban Protestantism it has little importance in public worship. Though we are intellectually aware that very much in the Bible is symbolic, we do not allow our life or worship to be deeply influenced by it. This may be a sign of spiritual maturity, or perhaps the reverse, but it does make it very difficult for us to understand a man like Ezekiel.

Ezekiel's training for the priesthood had familiarized him with every aspect of symbolism. In addition it is clear that he was a man for whom this method of expressing religious truth had a peculiar and special value. In our indifference to symbolism we often overlook the fact that there are some for whom it is indispensable, if they are to reach full communion with God. For such Ezekiel has a far deeper appeal than the other prophets of the Old Testament. Conversely those to whom symbolism means little will never find their favourite reading here. Since, however, God was well pleased to reveal Himself through this man, it is our duty to try and penetrate through the veil of symbolism to the truths underlying it. It may even be that as we make the effort we shall learn a deeper respect for this method of expressing the truth.

It is vital to remember this side of Ezekiel, as we read his prophecies, for we shall see that much in them which, if taken literally, seems difficult or offensive takes on a new meaning, if interpreted as predominantly symbolic.

The Exiles in Babylonia

We should not think of the exiles to whom Ezekiel prophesied as normal prisoners of war. Prisoners of war there were, many in 597 B.C., more after the destruction of Jerusalem in 586 B.C. These were slaves, whose fate depended on the whim of their captor or purchaser. The approximately ten thousand deportees (to whom we must probably add dependants) who were taken with Jehoiachin into exile were rather unreliable subjects of Nebuchadnezzar whom he had decided to move to another part of his dominions, where they could not get up to mischief.

A very few like Jehoiachin and his family were in company with other kinglets and princelings from subject territories, the "guests" of Nebuchadnezzar in or near Babylon itself. Though we cannot be sure, Jehoiachin's imprisonment was probably a precautionary measure when Zedekiah's rebellion broke out, though it may refer to his position from the first.

"The craftsmen and the smiths" (II Kings 24: 14) were for the most part held as a mobile labour force for work of national importance. We do not know enough of the conditions in Nebuchadnezzar's time to be able to say whether their skill was able to restrain their overseers' brutality.

From Jeremiah's letter (Jer. 29: 4–20) and from the general picture in Ezekiel it seems clear enough that the remainder of the exiles were settled in various centres in Babylonia with a great deal of freedom to live their lives as they wished. Probably the only important restriction placed on them was that they could not move to other centres, and it is questionable how far any of Nebuchadnezzar's subjects had unlimited freedom of movement. Our feeling that no effort was made to destroy their national existence is supported by the threefold reference to the elders of Judah in *Ezekiel* and by the general picture of the returning exiles given us in *Ezra*. In other words for the majority of those deported exile is a better word than captive.

To whom did Ezekiel Prophesy?

This study takes for granted that Ezekiel's prophetic activity was confined to the exiles, and that there is no evidence that he ever moved far from Tel-Abib. This has, however, been very strongly challenged in recent years. Many, including a few conservatives, maintain that ch. 4–24, either in whole or in major part, were spoken in Jerusalem, not in Babylonia, and that it is only from ch. 33 onwards that we have Ezekiel's prophecies to the exiles.[1]

The main reason for this view is superficially a valid one. If we except the prophecies against the nations, which in most cases were probably not communicated, except perhaps indirectly, to the nations concerned, we have no evidence for prophecy *about* persons rather than *to* them. There are cases where the prophetic message had to be sent by letter, e.g. II Chron. 21:12–15; Jer. 29; but there is no evidence that the message was first given orally to others. It is therefore at first sight strange enough that Ezekiel should act and speak a whole series of denunciations against Jerusalem to the exiles in Tel-Abib.

[1] The most plausible expression of this view may be found in Pfeiffer: *Introduction to the Old Testament*, pp. 535–541. It seems unnecessary to mention some of the more extreme modern views on the book.

It should be noted that there is no suggestion that the prophecies were to be written down and sent to Jerusalem. The
time needed speaks against it. It took six months for certain
news of the destruction of Jerusalem to reach Tel-Abib (33: 21
—see p. 118). Ezra under the most favourable conditions
("according to the good hand of his God upon him"), needed
three and a half months for the journey (Ezra 7: 9; 8: 31). The
length of Nehemiah's journey is not given, but the indications
are again that it will have lasted about the same time as Ezra's,
even though he had a royal escort and special papers.

Further, if Ezekiel had indeed sent his prophecies to Jerusalem, it seems strange that he did not seek to strengthen the
hands of lonely old Jeremiah there, or again that Jeremiah does
not even suggest that any such supporting prophecies ever
arrived from the far-distant exiles.

The ICC, holding the usual view that Ezekiel remained in
Babylonia, states (p. xxiii), "No doubt we find it difficult to
adjust ourselves to the position of a prophet in Babylonia hurl-
ing his denunciations at the inhabitants of Jerusalem across
700 miles of desert." I agree; it is not only difficult, but also
rather absurd.

When we examine the other arguments in favour of Ezekiel's
having prophesied in Jerusalem, we find them either very weak,
or quite capable of another explanation. Against the view is
above all that, as generally propounded, it involves alterations
in the order of the text, and makes Ezekiel a very clumsy writer
who has led generations of readers to false conclusions.

There is, however, an entirely satisfactory explanation of the
difficulty. Ezekiel was in fact prophesying *of* but not *to* Jerusalem. As Jer. 24 shows us, when Jehoiachin and his companions were led away captive, those left in Jerusalem put it
down to the peculiar sinfulness of the exiles. These probably
looked on it in the same light. The message of Jeremiah that
the exile was an act of grace on the part of God, and that the
real sinners had been left in Jerusalem for dire punishment, was
one that was hard to accept both in Jerusalem and in Babylonia. Until the exiles grasped that God had really brought
them into exile that He might make them the beginnings of a
renewed people, Ezekiel could not begin his task of preparing
them for the future. So during the last dark years of Jerusalem, before Nebuchadnezzar executed God's punishment to
the full on the city, Ezekiel had to explain to the exiles the
inner meaning of the agony that was going on in their father-
land. His message was not for those that were left in the city,
because, as Jeremiah had to say, there was no hope left for

them. But such was the effect of Ezekiel's work, that when temple and city went to the ground, and the end of Judah seemed to have come for all time, some at least of the exiles were willing to listen to Ezekiel and learn of him as he prepared a new generation for the return that God had promised when the seventy years had run their course.

In God's inspired record not merely the blessings of the righteous but also the fate of the sinner are recorded that we may learn both from the one and the other.

CHAPTER II

THE VISION OF GOD

THE THRONE OF GOD (1: 4–28)

In the height of the summer of 592 B.C. Ezekiel was transported in a trance (3: 12, 14) to the banks of the "river" Chebar, one of the main irrigation canals of Babylonia. Tel-abib (3: 15), his home, was in the immediate vicinity of the canal. He saw a great storm cloud coming towards him from the north (1: 4). As it drew nearer he saw that it was the chariot-throne of Jehovah borne by four cherubim. It is a basic Old Testament concept that the sovereignty of God is revealed both in His control of nature and of history. Ezekiel is to be the bearer of the message that the deportation of the exiles and the coming destruction of Jerusalem are God's act, so he is first given a vision of the mighty thunderstorm as a mere attendant on God's throne.

Why did the throne come from the north? The glory of Jehovah dwelt in Jerusalem (ch. 8–11), and the vision of its forsaking of the Temple had not yet been given. Jerusalem lay almost due west, and there was no need for God to take the long way round by Carchemish that the captives had had to follow. The desert was no obstacle to Him. One reason was doubtless to impress on the prophet to be that the shame and ignominy of the captives was not hidden from their God. He was willing to go the way that they had gone. More important than this was the Babylonian belief that their gods lived in the far north (Isa. 14: 13). If the chariot-throne came from the north, it meant that whatever gods might live there had been vanquished on the way. This is not to attribute to Ezekiel any real belief in these gods, but it was the sign that there was no power in heaven or on earth that could stay Jehovah on His triumphant way.

The bearers of the throne are the cherubim. It is frequently claimed by scholars that Ezekiel's description of them resembles the winged man-headed animals so often found as the guardians of Mesopotamian temples. I am far from convinced that this is so, but if they are correct, it simply means that not only has Jehovah defeated the gods of Babylon on their own ground, but He has also carried off their servants to be His slaves.

The cherubim, as an order of heavenly beings, are often mentioned in the Bible, but little is told us as to their functions. The differences in the description here and in Rev. 4 show us that in both cases we are dealing with a purely symbolic picture which need have no approximation to the reality. We cannot even assume that they were represented in approximately the same form on the mercy seat and in Solomon's temple. Note that in 41: 18, 19, possibly for ease in reproduction, the cherubim have only two faces. This supports the suggestion that we are dealing with symbolic representations of heavenly beings.[1]

Their appearance and their number, which again may well be symbolic, suggest that they are peculiarly the heavenly representatives of the earth. Modern man is strongly influenced by size, and even the Christian is inclined to depreciate the importance of the earth, a mere speck in the vast distances of space. This is especially the case if he is influenced by the old Greek dislike and suspicion of the material. But for the Old Testament this earth is the crown of God's creation and the especial revelation of His glory. So it is only fitting that His chariot-throne should be borne by beings who are particularly linked with God's creative and redemptive power here on earth.

It is doubtful whether much is to be gained by an attempt to puzzle out the details of the throne. The old rabbis declared that if anyone knew the secrets of the *merkabah*, he would know all the secrets of creation. This strongly suggests that the difficulties of the passage have little or nothing to do with the inadequacies of the English translation, but are due partly to Ezekiel's inability to describe what he saw with his spiritual eyes, partly to our lack of spiritual imagination. I shall content myself with elucidating some of the difficulties created by the translation and with pointing out some of the more obvious symbolic meanings.

Whether the ancients ever really thought of the world as square, I do not know, but the expression, the four corners, the four quarters, the four winds (37: 9) had become standard for the earth in its completeness; for this reason there are four cherubim (v. 5) forming a square, the representatives of the whole earth over which Jehovah holds sway. Theirs was "the likeness of a man" (v. 5), i.e. the human form predominated and they went upright. Their legs were straight (v. 7, RSV), the human aspect being once again stressed; there seems little meaning to be attached to their feet being like a calf's hoof. It

---

[1] Those interested will find a full discussion in Pember: *Earth's Earliest Ages*, pp. 168 *seq.* (15th edit., pp. 110 *seq.*).

seems probable that we are to understand that each cherub had two hands (v. 8); the four faces stress their nature as representatives of all living beings.

It is questionable whether the firmament (v. 22) is to be considered as supported on the wings of the cherubim. Rather their outstretched wings touching at the tips (v. 9) formed a protective square around the throne; such seems to be their role also in Rev. 4: 6. It is worth quoting the old rabbinic comment (Midrash Rabbah Shemoth § 23): "Man is exalted among creatures; the eagle is exalted among birds; the ox is exalted among domestic animals; the lion is exalted among wild beasts; and all of them have received dominion, and greatness has been given them, yet they are stationed below the chariot of the Holy One."

While the symbolic meaning of v. 12 is quite clear, it is not so obvious how we are to interpret the ability to go straight forward in any direction; the four-fold face is not paralleled in the rest of their bodies.

There can be no doubt that RV mg., RSV and Moffatt are correct in following LXX in v. 13, "In the midst of the living creatures there was something that looked like burning coals of fire . . ." (RSV); it is likely that Moffatt is correct in omitting v. 14 with some MSS. of LXX. The mysterious something probably symbolizes the Spirit of God, who vitalizes the cherubim.

The chariot-throne has wheels presumably just because it is a chariot-throne (cf. Dan. 7: 9), thereby indicating that His rule is everywhere, not merely in heaven. Since the chariot does not go on the ground but in the air, we are not to think of them as necessary for its movements. Their strange vitality and intelligence (the eyes) are to be attributed to their being part of the throne of God. In the presence of God even inanimate matter is permeated with life: "the spirit of life was in the wheels" (v. 20f., RV mg.). There is perfect unity between the living guardians and the inanimate wheels (v. 19).

The usual modern explanation of v. 16 is that the wheels, which formed another square within that formed by the cherubim, were seen by Ezekiel from an angle that made them seem to interlock. In any case their ability to go in any direction without turning (v. 17) is as mysterious as the similar power of the cherubim.

Above the cherubim and wheels Ezekiel saw a platform (firmament) supporting the throne, like ice or crystal (LXX omits terrible); this becomes the glassy sea of Rev. 4: 6. Just as the living creation is represented in the cherubim and inanimate nature in the wheels, so the glory of heaven is seen in the platform.

If anything the vision of God (vv. 26–28) is even more symbolic than what has preceded. Above the chariot is a "likeness of a throne" (v. 26), its colour reminiscent of the blue vault of heaven, and round it is the glory of the covenant rainbow (v. 28). The dimly seen figure is a combination of fire and glory. Since God made man in His own image, He deigns, when He appears to man in symbolic form, to appear to him in "a likeness as the appearance of a man."

THE VISION OF GOD (1:26 – 2:2)

The effect of the vision of God was that Ezekiel fell on his face (1: 28). Though it is not expressly stated, it seems clear enough that the vision had a paralysing effect on him, robbing him of all strength (cf. especially Dan. 8:17f.; 10:9ff.,15–19; Rev. 1: 17). He needed Divine power and energy before he could look on the glory—"the spirit" (2: 2) means the Spirit of God, but, as normally in the Old Testament, He is referred to impersonally, not personally, as normally in the New Testament.

It must be stressed that, however symbolic the vision, it was a real vision of God. It was not a vision of the chariot-throne, or of the cherubim, but of God. They all, in their manifold symbolism, are ultimately a revelation of God, for in the state He keeps we glimpse something of Him. To try and understand them as an end in itself is a misunderstanding of the purpose of the vision, and will bring little or no spiritual benefit.

It is quite common in popular piety to speak of seeing Christ. In its origin the phrase is probably a combination of certain passages of Scripture with the language of mysticism watered down to mean very little in particular. While it is undoubtedly granted to some children of God to have a vision of the risen Lord, such a vision is always a rare experience, which is bound to have the deepest imaginable effect on him who receives it. The hymn-writer was not sentimentalizing, when he wrote:

> Show me Thy face—one transient gleam
>   Of loveliness Divine,
> And I shall never think or dream
>   Of other love save Thine.

> All lesser light will darken quite,
>   All lower glories wane;
> The beautiful of earth will scarce
>   Seem beautiful again.

However popular the expression "seeing Christ" may have become with some to express a spiritual awareness of His presence, we would do well to reserve it for experiences comparable with those described in the Bible. Above all it should not be used for the ability some possess of summoning up a mental picture *of their own creating* of our Lord. To see God means to be transformed.

It should be noted and pondered that, so far as we have any record, it is not to man prostrate and weak before Him that God gives His prophetic message, but to man standing on his feet and strengthened by the Spirit. There are times and seasons, when the child of God will be found prostrate before the Lord, but when he is to be God's "fellow-worker," he is to stand upon his feet. "It is man erect, man in his manhood, with whom God will have fellowship and with whom He will speak" (A. B. Davidson). God's service is a willing and rational service, not the service of automata.

CHAPTER III

GOD'S SERVANT

Ezekiel's Commissioning (2:3 – 3:14)

EZEKIEL is addressed as "Son of man." This cannot be linguistically equated with the title "The Son of Man," which our Lord used of Himself. Something of the meaning of the former may be in the latter, but the latter far transcends it, involving as it does a self-identification with the Messianic figure of Dan. 7: 13 and a claim to be the one true and representative man. A more idiomatic rendering of Son of man would be "child of man"; it really means no more than "man"; it stresses his insignificance compared to the glory he has just seen, but it is in no way depreciatory, for man, in spite of his fall, is and remains the climax of God's creating.

The story of the actual commissioning gives the impression of being spread over a period of time. In a trance-vision "time" takes on a meaning rather different to that which it generally bears; it is no longer "clock time," open to human measurement. But however the passage of time is to be measured, God, as always, instructs His servant step by step. The whole burden, the whole message, does not become his at once. He has to adapt himself and assimilate before the message is continued. Why, even the explanation of the special form of his prophetic activity is delayed to a slightly later season (3: 15–21). This is always God's way, though in normal experience the learning is spread over a "longer" time.

In 2: 3–7 Ezekiel is introduced to those to whom he was to prophesy, "nations that are rebellious" (v. 3, RV), i.e. both Judah and Israel. The term "Judah" is very seldom used in Ezekiel, and where it is, apart perhaps from 8:17, it means the Southern Kingdom as distinct from the Northern, or the tribe of Judah as distinct from the other tribes. Normally, as the context shows again and again, "the House of Israel" and "the children of Israel" refer in the first place to the citizens of the Southern Kingdom, whether in exile or in Judæa; when it is otherwise the context makes it clear. This choice of name is due to two obvious reasons. In exile the captives who were removed with Jehoiachin will to some extent—how far we do

27

not know—have come into contact with the descendants of captives from the North, and the message was intended for them as well. Then Ezekiel, like Jeremiah, was of the tribe of Levi, and so the use of Israel was the more natural for both of them (cf. also p. 131f.).[1] God's opening charge did not fully reveal how Ezekiel's message would be received, but it was made clear enough that great difficulties were to be expected.

There follows a symbolic picture of the source of Ezekiel's message and inspiration (2:8–3:3). No such picture is to be found in the earlier prophets, for it would have ill-fitted the relationship in which they knew themselves to be with God, but for all that Ezekiel's picture fits all prophecy. It may have been Ezekiel's priestly outlook that made him more conscious of the distance between him and God, and hence made this symbolic picture more suited to him. It strikingly illustrates the union of the Divine and human in the prophetic message. The message is clearly Divine, from God, for the roll is already written, and that "within and without," i.e. there is no room for any additions by the prophet himself. But the prophet does not merely take it with him to Tel-Abib and read it to the exiles. He has to eat it, to assimilate it, to make it a living part of himself; this is the human part of the message. The effect of the assimilation is interestingly indicated in 3: 3, 14. First the word of Jehovah is received and is very sweet. But as it is assimilated and becomes part of the prophet, it dominates him and makes him share on a human level Jehovah's attitude towards a sinful people (cf. Jer. 6: 11, especially the punctuation in RSV). The roll contained only "lamentations, mourning and woe" because Ezekiel received a virtual re-commissioning (33: 1–20) before he began his work of building up and comforting.

Once Ezekiel receives God's message, it is made clear to him that it will be refused, and that deliberately and without excuse, though presumably 3:11 held out some hope that some might accept. Though Ezekiel's message was to the exiles in general, it was to be spoken particularly to those among whom he lived (3: 11), and this was underlined by the Spirit's returning him to his home (3:12–15).

"The spirit lifted me up" might be interpreted in a purely natural sense, were it not for 8: 3. The two passages must surely be interpreted identically, and a purely natural inter-

---

[1] Though Israel in Jeremiah normally means or includes the Southern Kingdom, there are passages where it must either mean those left in the area of the Northern Kingdom, or the descendants of those who had gone into exile from Samaria.

pretation is excluded in the latter. We shall deal with the deeper implications of the "levitation" when discussing ch. 4. For the moment it is sufficient to say that since few, if any, will argue for a literal physical levitation, we were justified in using the term trance for the whole experience of 1:3–3:14.

EZEKIEL THE WATCHMAN (3: 15–21)

It is often said that "God's appointing is God's enabling." This is true enough, but life is not as simple as all that. The application of God's words to human sin and need is more than "and it was in my mouth as honey for sweetness," or "in bitterness, in the heat of my spirit." When Ezekiel returns to his familiar surroundings and looks on them with new eyes, he sits astonied (RV, RSV "overwhelmed") for seven days. He needs time to get adjusted to the new circumstances.

In the seven days symbolism breaks through again. Seven days were the time of mourning for the dead (cf. Gen. 50: 10; Num. 19:11; Job 2:13); Ezekiel is a new man, for the Spirit has entered into him, but the week of impurity for the corpse of the old must pass before he begins his work. Seven days were the period of consecration for the priest (Lev. 8: 33). Ezekiel is to carry out his priestly work as a prophet, so before his work begins the week of consecration must elapse.

When the period of waiting ended, God made his commission clearer to Ezekiel. He was to be especially a watchman. This was not an entirely new name for a prophet. Watchman may be so used in Isa. 21: 6; 62: 6; and Hab. 2: 1, though such an interpretation is not necessary and at least in one case improbable. It is rather more likely in Isa. 52: 8, and virtually certain in Jer. 6: 17. But the very paucity of references is evidence enough that it was neither a normal name nor function for the prophet. But in Ezekiel we find it both at the beginning of the prophet's activity and at his re-commissioning (33: 1–9). Evidently it expressed a feature of his work that either did not appear or was not prominent in that of his predecessors.

In the old dispensation a most important part of the priest's work, though we often forget it, was that of "pastoral oversight." It was the priest's task to try and see that the Law was known and kept (cf. Lev. 10: 11; Deut. 24: 8; Mal. 2 :7; II Chron. 17: 7ff.). Ezekiel is not to be merely God's spokesman to the people in general; he is to be God's messenger to the individual in particular. The use of the singular in this passage is not merely an example of the vivid concreteness of Hebrew, but does definitely envisage Ezekiel's speaking to individuals as he sees their work and daily life. The fact that only his public ministry has been preserved for us does not nullify this conclusion.

It has been said epigrammatically, " Jeremiah was a prophet who happened to be a priest; Ezekiel was a priest who happened to be a prophet." If we allow for the inevitable exaggeration of epigrams, this is very true. Though Ezekiel is a genuine prophet, yet he is carrying out his priestly functions by so acting; he is above all the pastoral prophet caring for the souls of the individuals. This explains, if we accept the suggestion on p. 16, why the call should have come just when he was thirty (1: 1).

CHAPTER IV

THE FIRST PROPHECIES

A Prophet Restrained (3: 22–27)

To our surprise we find that almost immediately after his commissioning—the interval between 1: 2 and 8: 1 interpreted in the light of 4: 5f. will only permit of a very brief time—Ezekiel is instructed to shut himself up at home, which he either is not to leave, or will not be able to; in addition he is either not to speak, or will not be able to (v. 26). The probable reason is given in v. 25, unless with RSV and Moffatt we follow, quite unnecessarily, the LXX and read "and cords will be placed upon you."

"They shall lay bands upon thee" should hardly be taken literally; it represents rather the extreme and bitter opposition of his fellow-exiles to his prophesying. This was probably due to the incident described in Jer. 29: 21–23. It should be obvious that Nebuchadnezzar's drastic punishment was not inflicted on Ahab and Zedekiah for their immorality, even though that is why God caused it to be inflicted. They had prophesied the early return of Jehoiachin and the exiles to Jerusalem, which to Nebuchadnezzar meant a prophecy of his own collapse; not unreasonably he treated it as an incitement to rebellion and as high treason. The false prophets' execution will have been associated with real peril for others of the exiles, so we have an adequate explanation for the bitter hostility that greeted the appearance of a new prophet.

The immediate result was another trance vision (vv. 22f.) in which God commanded Ezekiel to refrain from public ministry. He would match restraint (v. 25) with restraint (4: 8) and unwillingness to hear with silence (v. 26), though from time to time Ezekiel would be able to speak (v. 27).

This is a suitable point for considering a major problem of interpretation in the earlier chapters of Ezekiel: are we to take certain statements literally, or are we to consider them as metaphors and symbols? Ezekiel's dumbness is mentioned again 24: 27; 29: 21; 33: 22, but in other passages he is shown as speaking normally, e.g. 14: 4; 17: 2f., 12; 19: 1; 20: 3, and many others. It could be urged that in all these cases God had suspended the dumbness as promised in 3: 27. But in fact

31

there is never any hint that this was the case. Passages like
8:1; 14: 1–4; 20:1 suggest that the elders expected him to
be able to speak (cf. p. 40).

In ch. 4 Ezekiel is described as lying on his side for 390 days
—for this figure see below—bound with cords (v. 8), which
might mean some form of paralysis, but all the time pressing
the siege of Jerusalem with his model (4: 1–3) and doing a
number of actions (4: 9 – 5: 4) which seem to be physically
incompatible with his lying on his side. Every form of dog-
matism is out of place here, but once we are forced to realize
that 4:1–5:4 cannot be interpreted literally in all its details,
it is not unreasonable to remember Ezekiel's extreme use of
symbolism, and to allow for a metaphorical or symbolical
element in the language used. So far as 4:1–5:4 are concerned
we leave the application of our principle to the next section.
It seems probable that Ezekiel's dumbness was no actual
inability to speak, but a refusal to speak on ordinary matters
with those who had refused to hear him as God's messenger,
combined with a relative rarity in Divine revelations. In addition, of course, those who had refused to listen to Ezekiel,
when he came to them, had now to eat humble pie and go to
him, if they wished to hear the Divine message.

PREACHING BY SYMBOLS (4:1 – 5:4)

It would seem that the use of symbolic actions by prophets goes
right back to the early days of prophecy. A few examples from
prophets true and false are I Sam. 15: 27f.; I Kings 11: 29ff.;
22: 11; II Kings 13: 14–19. Behind these actions lie the deep
convictions of more primitive men that words and actions are
significant, and that by doing something similar to what you
prophesy, you are helping forward the fulfilment and making
it more. certain. Note how hate against Jeremiah flared up
(Jer. 20: 1f.) after the symbolic action of the breaking of the
pot (Jer. 19: 1–13). I am not suggesting that the true prophets
believed this, but that they knew that such symbolic actions
made their words the more impressive. When we come to the
written prophets there seems to be a change in the reason for
symbolism. The false prophets still kept it up for the old
reasons, e.g. Jer. 28: 10f., but men like Isaiah and Jeremiah
used it when they could no longer obtain a hearing for the
spoken word, e.g. Isa. 20: 2f.; Jer. 19: 1f., 10f. Such actions
not merely tickled men's curiosity, but filled them with a sense
of awe as they superstitiously believed that the prophet was
doing things that would bring evil on men.

We can easily understand then the excitement in Tel-Abib as the news went round that Ezekiel, who had not been seen outside his house for days, was acting in a way calculated to bring disaster on Jerusalem. Daily the group inside the door of the house watching the silent prophet lying on the floor with his model would grow, until they were ready to hear the Divine explanation of his actions (5: 5–7: 27), if indeed an explanation was necessary.

Between 1: 2 and 8: 1 are exactly a year and two months. The Jewish year is a lunar year of 354 days, the months being alternatively 30 and 29 days in length. So we are dealing with a period of 413 days. If it was a leap year, which today comes round about twice in five years, and which is formed by the insertion of an extra 29-day month, we can extend the period to 442 days. It is therefore clear that, if it were an ordinary year, the figures of 4: 5f. must be looked on as not consecutive but concurrent. Even if we assume a leap year we must allow for the seven days of 3: 16 and the unspecified period of 3: 22 as well as the day or two that Ezekiel would have needed to make his preparations. This just barely allows the 390 days for Israel and the 40 for Judah to be consecutive, so in the light of 4: 9 we shall probably be safe in assuming that in either case the 390 days and the 40 days are to be taken as concurrent. Obviously, if we follow LXX, as do Moffatt and NBC, and read 190 in 4: 5, 9, this argument has no validity.

If this is so, all element of the completely literal vanishes. We can picture Ezekiel at one time lying on his left side, at another on his right, at another making his strange bread, at another shaving his head and dealing with the hair. Indeed at night, when no inquisitive visitors were to be expected, he may have slept like any normal mortal.

The tile (4: 1—RSV "brick") is obviously a freshly made Babylonian clay brick, on which a sketch of Jerusalem could easily be cut. Whether the siege works were to be cut in the clay as well, or whether they were to be separate clay models, the Hebrew does not really make clear. On the whole the latter seems more probable, for it was obviously intended to be clearly understood by any chance visitor without any explanation on Ezekiel's part. Indeed "thou shalt lay siege against it" (4: 3—RSV "press the siege") may well indicate the gradual moving of the models nearer and nearer to the doomed city.

The symbolism of Ezekiel lying on his side presents no particular difficulty. The left side is chosen for Israel, for one standing facing east in Palestine had Israel to the north, i.e. to the left and Judah to the right. The immobility and cords

C

(4: 8) symbolize the conditions of exile. "To bear the iniquity of" means to bear the punishment of, though this must be taken purely symbolically; he was bearing in symbol the punishment they were actively suffering. But so far as I know no certain sense has ever been made of the figures. We need have no difficulty that they are to be concurrent, i.e. that the last 40 of the 390 were to be on his right side, for the two kingdoms were now in exile together. But why 40 and 390?

It is claimed on the basis of 29: 11–14 that Ezekiel thought that the exile would last 40 years. Even assuming that that is a correct interpretation of the passage, we must not forget that the prophecy against Egypt is dated over five years later. If the two passages are legitimately to be brought together, it would only mean that 40 is no more than a round number. There is no intrinsic objection to this, but it seems impossible so to interpret 390. In addition there can be no doubt that Ezekiel knew Jeremiah's prophecies (25: 12 and 29: 10). Since the same figure of 70 years is used on two occasions some years apart, when looking forward to the same event, it is clear that it is meant to be a round figure, but as we might expect it is an accurate one. From the victory at Carchemish (605 B.C.), when Babylonian rule over the West began, to the capture of Babylon by Cyrus (538 B.C.) is 67 years. The actual captivity of those taken away with Jehoiachin was 59 years, and of those that stayed in Jerusalem until its capture (586 B.C.) 48 years.

It may be that the LXX preserves the original reading in vv. 5, 9, i.e. 190. This would represent in round figures the 185 years from the destruction of Samaria (722 B.C.) to the fall of Babylon. Since there is no simple way in which the change of reading could have come about, and there are two verses involved, not merely one, it is far more likely that the Greek was deliberately changed to suit the apparently obvious meaning of the passage.

It is more likely that the figure 40 was chosen by God as being less than the total of Babylonian lordship, and being at the same time reminiscent of the 40 years in the wilderness. If we subtract the 40 from the 390, for the last period was shared by both kingdoms equally, 350 represents in round numbers the period from Jeroboam, son of Nebat, when Israel split from Judah, down to Ezekiel's own time. I put forward this suggestion with diffidence, but it does suit the thoroughly symbolic setting.[1]

Ezekiel's diet during this period contains a double picture. The confining of his food to about 12 ozs. of "bread" and his

[1] See Additional Note at end of chapter.

drink to about 1¾ pints of water a day is a grim picture of siege conditions. The actual nature of the food, however, not merely reproduces siege conditions but points to the impurity of the exile that is to follow (4: 13). Instead of the normal fuel of the East, cow's dung, man's dung, impure and defiling (cf. Deut. 23: 12ff.), must be used, though here God has pity on the frailty of His prophet. The mixture of grains and seeds not merely vividly expresses the necessity of the besieged to eat what they could get, but also was almost certainly defiling, at least for those like Ezekiel, who took ceremonial purity seriously. We can infer this from commandments like Lev. 19: 19; Deut. 22: 9ff.

Finally, doubtless when the 390 days were drawing to an end, Ezekiel startled the group of onlookers by shaving head and beard with a sword. Shaving of the head, though forbidden in the Law (Lev. 19:27f.; 21:5; Deut. 14:1), was a universal sign of mourning practised widely in Israel (Isa. 3: 24; 22:12; Mic. 1: 16; Jer. 16: 6, etc.). Ezekiel's use of a sword as razor left no doubt in the onlookers' minds what the reason of the mourning was. The weighing and dividing of the hair looks to prophecies like Jer. 15: 2 and cf. Ezek. 5: 12; 6: 12, and stresses the Divine supervision of the doom.

5: 2ff. describe Ezekiel's actions when the 390 days are past. One-third of the hair is to be burnt on the brick that served as the model of Jerusalem; one-third is to be chopped small; one-third is to be thrown to the winds. It was the message of both Jeremiah (24: 8ff.) and Ezekiel that those left in Jerusalem with Zedekiah were the worst of the people. That probably explains the difficult words (5: 4): "therefrom (RV) shall a fire come forth into all the house of Israel." Those few who managed to escape and link up with the exiles already in Babylonia would only prove a curse to them.

It should not be forgotten that these symbolic prophecies of Ezekiel were not the foretelling of the end of a siege already begun. They were given about four years before Zedekiah's revolt ever broke out. They are a preparation of the exiles for the final tragedy that was yet to come.

THE COMING DOOM OF JERUSALEM (5:5 – 7:27)

It is of little or no importance whether we think of these prophecies being given during the later part of the time of the symbolic actions, or whether they were given afterwards. In any case by his methods Ezekiel had won the interest of the exiles, and he seems to have been treated with respect from then on, cf. 8: 1; 14: 1; 20: 1.

The prophecy in 5: 5–17 is little more than a commentary on the symbolic actions. Note that the judgment is coming more for the past wickedness of the people than for the sin of those in Jerusalem at the time. This is a note we find repeatedly, cf. II Kings 24: 3f.; Jer. 15: 4, etc. Josiah's reformation had come too late. It only served to show that the rot had gone too deep. Since God had already removed the good figs (Jer. 24), only judgment dire and absolute could await the remainder. This too, and not merely that he was not directly addressing the people in Jerusalem, helps to explain his apparent lack of humanity, which so many have remarked on.

In 38: 12 Palestine is called the navel of the earth (RV mg.), but it is very doubtful whether this and 5: 5 is intended to be taken in the literal way in which medieval map-makers and indeed some moderns have understood it. The remarkable feature of Jerusalem is how isolated it can be from the life that pulses round it. God set Israel where it could work out God's will for it, but where in turn Arabian and Canaanite, Egyptian, Hittite and Babylonian, Greek and Roman brought their influences and civilizations and might in turn have been influenced (and some influence there was) had Israel remained loyal to its God. The thought of v. 7 is illustrated by Jer. 2: 10f.; the religions of Israel's neighbours might not be admirable, but at least they were loyal to them.

It is easy for us to criticize the spiritual blindness of the majority of the people, who could not believe the message of the coming destruction of city and temple, but 5: 9 should make us temper our judgment. There was no precedent to prepare for it.

The second of the prophecies (ch. 6) is an explanation of the preceding. It explains that the sin that was bringing destruction on Jerusalem was above all a religious one, the worship of Jehovah as though He had been but a nature god, with all the appurtenances and ritual of nature worship, a worship which the prophets quite simply call idolatry and Baal worship. It had come into Israel in the period of the Judges and had never been eradicated. It had been checked by men like Samuel, David, Asa and Hezekiah. But Manasseh in his long 55-year reign had deliberately opened every door to it, and now only the fires of exile could burn it out. The prophecy is addressed specially to the mountains of Israel, for it was especially the hill-tops that had housed the semi-pagan sanctuaries. The following chapters repeatedly describe this popular religion from various aspects.

It is almost certain that in v. 9 in place of "I have been

broken" we should read with some of the old versions (and so
RV mg., RSV): "when I have broken their whorish heart." To
clap one's hands and stamp one's feet (v. 11) is a sign of deep
emotion and rejoicing (cf. 25: 6); so instead of "alas!" we
should render the Hebrew "Ha!" Ezekiel is called on to re-
joice that the accumulated evil of centuries is to be swept away.
In v. 14 we have probably a case of one of the commonest of
all scribal errors in the Old Testament, the confounding of D
and R; render, "from the wilderness to Riblah" (RSV), i.e. from
South to North (cf. Num. 34: 11).

This section ends (ch. 7) with a dirge over the land for the
coming destruction. The language is broken and difficult, but
the general sense is clear. On the analogy of other passages it
is very likely that the silver and gold in v. 19 does not refer so
much to the inability of their riches to help them, but rather to
the helplessness of their idols of silver and gold. Note "doom"
(RV), not "morning," in v. 7.

"THEY SHALL KNOW THAT I AM THE LORD."

"Thou shalt (ye shall, they shall) know that I am the LORD"
is the most characteristic expression of Ezekiel. It occurs in
this simple form no less than 54 times and with some expansion
another 18 times. This knowledge is always connected either
with the judgments of God or with His acts of grace; it is
probably only due to the greatly predominating stress on God's
judgment in Ezekiel that the majority of the passages fall into
the former category.

From the similar Ex. 3: 6, and from Ex. 6: 7 the expression
"I am Jehovah" occurs in various settings from time to time
throughout the Old Testament. It must not be compared with
Ex. 3: 14, for the verb is not expressed in Hebrew in "I am
Jehovah"; it is not the existence of Jehovah that is being
stressed, but the identity of the speaker and of Jehovah. It
would have been in fact better to say the identity of the actor
and Jehovah, for normally, and invariably in Ezekiel, this
phrase is used in connexion with Jehovah's actions.

Had Israel been a theologically and philosophically inclined
people, we might have said that 'elohim (= the uniquely mighty
one, i.e. God) represented the God of natural theology, the God
whose attributes we can discover from nature around us, while
Jehovah stands for the God of revelation. Though that would
be an overstatement, it yet remains true that Jehovah meant
for the Israelite God as He had made Himself known in redemption and covenant. Men to whom God has so revealed

Himself, even though He had announced Himself as I WILL BE THAT I WILL BE (Ex. 3: 14, RV mg.), are always tempted to believe that the revelation is completed and their understanding of it perfect. Even for the Christian, though the revelation is now complete, his understanding of it is never perfect. There is always the temptation to turn the historic acts of revelation into the abstractions of theology.

In Ezekiel's day men were quite sure what Jehovah would and would not, could and could not do. The coming destruction of Jerusalem and the temple and the building of a new people in exile meant the turning over of a fresh leaf in the book of God's revelation, and Ezekiel is stressing that the one who is bringing calamity and fresh grace upon them is the same one who brought them out of Egypt and made a covenant with them at Sinai. We must note though that this fresh knowledge of God was not to come by a fresh study of the revelation of the past or by a renewed speaking through His prophets, but before all else by His acts. Our God is not merely a God who speaks but also a God who acts, and His words have to be interpreted in the framework of His mighty acts.

ADDITIONAL NOTE TO CH. IV

At the time when this chapter was first written I did not have access to the ICC volume on Ezekiel. Its comments on 4: 4ff. are too important to be ignored, but as they only tended to confirm me in my interpretation, it seemed best to leave the text as it stood.

Cooke follows LXX, as against the Hebrew and other versions, in reading 190 instead of 390 in vv. 5, 9, though from his remark on pp. 50, 52, he evidently does not consider that this figure comes from Ezekiel himself. He explains it as being the period in round numbers from the deportation by Tiglath-pileser in 734 B.C. (II Kings 15: 29) to Ezekiel plus the forty years of Judah's punishment. To justify his choice he uses three arguments:

(a) "It is incredible that any man could lie prostrate on one side for such a length of time [390 days] and retain his senses" (p. 52). This argument loses much of its force because he interprets Ezekiel's dumbness as "abstaining from the prophetic task of being *a reprover*" (p. 48); why should he then insist on the literal interpretation of his immobility? In addition he moves vv. 4–8 after 3: 24, separating Ezekiel's immobility from the other symbolic actions in 4: 1–5 : 4.

(b) He sees the impossibility of explaining the change from

190 to 390 and considers that it was deliberate. Just as with the Greek MSS. of the New Testament, the Hebrew MSS. of the Old show the type of error that scribes were always prone to. This is more than normally the case in Ezekiel because of the extreme difficulty of much of the language; a comparison of the Hebrew and LXX shows that not infrequently marginal comments have been incorporated into the text. There are a few deliberate changes for reverential reasons and the like; the rabbis acknowledge this in 8: 17. There is, however, no evidence anywhere for the type of deliberate alteration Cooke presupposes. It is the more incredible, since it would almost certainly have been made after the LXX translation of Ezekiel, which cannot be much earlier than 150 B.C.

(c) He thinks that the scribe responsible misunderstood v. 4 and thought it referred to Israel's sinning, not to its punishment, and so put in a figure to reach back to the disruption of the kingdom in the time of Jeroboam. We are apt to look on the disruption as a punishment on Solomon, but God permitted the disruption not merely as a punishment for Solomon's idolatry, but also because the North wished to break away, and it was His punishment on Israel as well. For Ezekiel the North separated from God's sanctuary on Zion and from the Davidic king of God's choice, was in semi-exile from the time of the disruption.

CHAPTER V

ICHABOD[1]

Jehovah Abandons His Temple (8:1 – 11:25)

By the end of his prophesying through symbolic actions
(4:1–5:4) Ezekiel had become a highly respected member
of his community. This may have been partly due to
his aristocratic, priestly origin, but probably still more to the
nature of his prophecy. I earlier suggested (p. 31) that it was
fear that led to his initial rejection. The leaders of the exiles
will soon have realized that Ezekiel's message was one that
Nebuchadnezzar would welcome rather than punish. At any
rate a year and two months (8: 1) after his inaugural vision, we
find the elders of Judah sitting before Ezekiel in his house.
This implies that they had come to discover the will of Jehovah,
and were sitting in the respectful position of scholars to learn
from Ezekiel.

Ezekiel's visit to Jerusalem described in this section was
purely in the spirit; there is no real suggestion that his body
was carried there. This is indicated by the nature of what he
saw, for much cannot be taken literally, and by actions which
would hardly have been physically possible (e.g. 8: 8), and even
more by the definite statement in 8: 3; 11: 24 (cf. 3: 12, 14).
This is no abstract point, for we shall see below that much, if
not all, of the vision in ch. 8 is to be taken symbolically, which
could hardly be the case, if Ezekiel had been physically in
Jerusalem. Though it is not stated, it is likely that Ezekiel
spoke aloud during the vision, giving the elders some idea of
what he was passing through; thus they will have been a
guarantee that it was a genuine vision and not mere invention,
when the whole came to be told (11: 25). Whether, as some
think, the purpose of the elders' visit was in some way connected
with the theme of the vision, we cannot now know.

In 8: 2 we should read with LXX "the appearance of a man"
(so RSV—the same consonants in older Hebrew MSS.). It is
the same symbolic vision of God as in 1: 27. Since we are
dealing with a vision, there is no reason for finding difficulty in
the fact that Ezekiel's transportation to Jerusalem is first
ascribed to the hand of God and then to the Spirit (8: 3).

[1] 'The glory is departed' (I Sam. 4: 21f.).

To get a clear picture of what follows, it must be borne in mind that in one major detail Solomon's temple differed widely from Zerubbabel's and Herod's. On the temple-mount from north to south lay three groups of buildings, the temple, the royal palace, the House of the Forest of Lebanon. The first two had each its own court, while the whole complex was surrounded by "the great court."[1] In other words, the temple had only one court that strictly belonged to it. The incidents seen by Ezekiel took place partly in the temple court proper, partly in the adjacent great court. I understand that what took place in the great court symbolized those cults and practices that had not the official sanction of the temple authorities.

When Ezekiel arrived in spirit in the temple court, the glory of God had already left the holy of holies, and he saw it first in some unspecified part of the court (8: 4).

THE IDOLATRY OF JERUSALEM (8: 5–18)

It is usually assumed that Ezekiel's vision represents the actual and mainly public idolatry of Jerusalem in the time of Zedekiah, but there are apparently insuperable difficulties in accepting this view. An open reversion to the forms of religion swept away by Josiah's reformation would have meant public apostasy, but neither in II Kings 23:31–25:26; II Chron. 36: 1–21, nor in Jeremiah is there any indication of this. The references to idolatry in Jer. 2 are to the period before Josiah's reformation was carried through. We find idolatry in Jer. 7: 16–18, but we get the impression rather of a popular drift back to the old ways, as they were under Manasseh, rather than of an official reintroduction of the old. This is borne out by Jer. 44: 15–23, for v. 18 is incompatible with an open resumption of the old heathen rites of the "divine mother" in the time of Zedekiah. So it is much more likely that we have here a mainly symbolic picture of the false beliefs that held sway in Jerusalem, though they may have had only a restricted public expression.

In fact the four forms of idolatrous worship presented do represent what we know from other passages to have been the false religious tendencies in the century and a half before the exile, though in the last the priests seem to have gone further than any before them.

(1) The Image of Jealousy (vv. 3, 5). That we are dealing with popular religion seems to be shown by the image's being *outside* the north gate (see RV or RSV of v. 5), and so in the

[1] See the diagram accompanying the article "Temple," in *International Standard Bible Encyclopaedia* or *Hastings' Dictionary of the Bible*.

great court.   That an image in connexion with Jehovah worship
is intended is virtually certain (cf. Ex. 20: 4f., Deut. 4: 23f.,
5: 8f., which are shown by the context to refer primarily to
images of Jehovah, or in connexion with Him), but in view of
the fact that the archaeologist has yet to discover an image of
Jehovah, or indeed of any male god, in any undoubtedly
Israelite setting,[1] though images of goddesses are common, it
seems more likely that an image or symbol of Asherah, the
mother-goddess of the Canaanites, conceived of as Jehovah's
wife (cf. I Kings 15: 13 RV mg., II Kings 21: 7 RV, etc.) is
intended.[2]

The reference here will be to that popular Canaanization of
Jehovah worship that was the curse of Israel from the time of
the Judges and was stigmatized by the prophets as merely
Baal-worship.   It bore the same relation to the revelation of
Sinai as popular Roman-Catholicism does to the religion of the
New Testament.   The position of the image just outside the
most popular gateway to the temple court shows that this
debased conception of Jehovah dominated the popular mind
but had not yet been reinstated into the public rites of the
temple, whence it had been removed by Josiah.

(2) The Worship of the Elders (vv. 6–12).   It is usually taken
for granted that the mention of animal worship refers to
Egyptian idolatry, introduced, perhaps on political grounds,
early in the reign of Jehoiakim.   But apart from a few cults
Egyptian religion was not for export, and if there had been a
cult brought in for political reasons, it would probably have
been that of Amon or perhaps Osiris.   ICC (p. 94) points out
rightly that certain aspects of Babylonian religion would fit
the description equally well.   But "all the idols of the house
of Israel" (v. 10) suggests that any such interpretation is too
narrow, and "every man in his chambers of imagery" (v. 12)
makes a purely literal understanding dangerous, as indeed does
the way that Ezekiel gains access to their worship.   The precise
figure too of seventy contrasted with the "about five and
twenty" of v. 16 suggests that it is to be taken symbolically as
meaning that all, or virtually all, the elders were involved in
this idolatry, whereas only a few of the priests had taken the
final step of apostasy.

It is probable that Ezekiel is referring to all the foreign cults,
especially from Assyria and Babylon that had poured into the
country in the time of Ahaz and Manasseh, but which had

[1] See G. E. Wright: *The Old Testament against its Environment*, p. 24f.

[2] A good example of such debased worship was revealed in the papyri discovered at Elephantine or Yeb, see any good *recent* work on Biblical
archaeology.

influenced mainly the ruling classes.   Ezekiel's picture of them
is probably intended rather to express his disgust of them than
to describe them accurately.   Once Judah had learnt to worship
other gods beside Jehovah and even as His superiors in power,
it needed more than a superficial reformation to eradicate the
conceptions that lay behind it and the memories of the worship
in which many of the older ones will have been reared.   The
combination of secrecy with defiant despair, "The Lord seeth us
not; the Lord hath forsaken the land" (v. 12 RV mg., cf. 9:9
RV mg.) reminds us of the mentality of Jer. 44:18.   They were
still ashamed to go back openly on the covenant made under
Josiah, but they had opened their hearts to the idolatries and
memories of the past.

(3) The Wailing for Tammuz (vv. 13, 14).   The very fact
that it is the women, the most conservative element in oriental
religious life, who are seen wailing for Tammuz, is the best
refutation of the suggestion that we have to do with a recent
importation from Babylonia.   We are dealing here with a popular form of the vegetation myth found in Old Testament times
everywhere from Canaan to Babylonia, in which the god of
vegetation, here Tammuz, died in the summer heat and came
back to life with the coming of the rains.   Ezekiel's vision was
about August, when Palestine is at its most parched and burnt
from the summer heat, and green is to be seen only where there
is running water or irrigation.   Doubtless the name may have
been a new importation, but the cult was ancient.

The previous idolatries were firstly a degrading of Jehovah
and secondly an admission of the gods of the conquering lands
beside Him as objects of worship.   Here, however, there is pure
nature worship, in which the covenant of Sinai could find little,
if any, place.   We may gather that in the average home the
women had little real share in religion.   The inevitable result
was that they all too often were the transmitters of the worst
superstitions and beliefs of the neighbours of Israel.

(4) Sun Worship (vv. 15–18).   The approximately twenty-
five sun-worshippers were, as we may infer from where they
were standing, either priests or Levites; from 9:6 we see they
were of senior rank.   Here was not merely debasing of Jehovah
worship, or the linking of it to other cults, but, as the position
of the worshippers shows, a deliberate rejection of Jehovah.
They were worshipping Shamash, the Babylonian sun-god,
thereby recognizing that the gods of Babylon had defeated
Jehovah, who could no longer help them.   With their idolatry
went not merely social violence but also some supreme insult
to Jehovah: it is expressed in the words, "and lo, they put the

branch to My nose," as a valid Rabbinic tradition preserves
v. 17, which was changed to its present form out of respect to
God.   The "branch" is generally explained by reference to the
ritual of the Persian honouring of the sun.   This has, however,
no real connexion with the sun-worship of Babylonia, nor is
there any evidence that any such ritual was there used.   In
addition it is not even certain that reference is being made to
the actual sun-worship.   It is better to follow Jewish tradition
and see in the word *zemorah* not a branch but some act of
peculiar insult or obscenity.   From this part of the vision we
can see the justice of Jeremiah's condemnation of the priests
(Jer. 5: 31; 6: 13).

THE JUDGMENT OF JERUSALEM (9:1 – 10:2)

This vision is not symbolically descriptive like the preceding,
but is symbolically predictive, for Zedekiah's rebellion against
Nebuchadnezzar had not even broken out yet.

The instruments of judgment are obviously angels, though
they are always called men.   It has been maintained that their
number mirror the seven planet-gods of Babylonia, the one with
the writer's ink-horn corresponding to Nebo. Any such assumption is entirely needless, for in a vision where symbolism plays
such a part seven is an obvious number.   But, if the suggestion
has truth in it, it would mean no more than what we said of
the cherubim (p. 22), i.e. that Jehovah is the Lord of whatever
"gods" there may be.

The angels were armed with "clubs" (9: 2—so ICC, which
compares it with Jer. 51: 20ff, where the same word is used, cf.
RV mg. and RSV *ad loc.*).   The slaughter was not to be indis-
criminate, which is perhaps why angel instruments rather than
a general catastrophe are used for the judgment.   The apostasy
was not absolute, and so a mark of safety was to be placed on
the foreheads of God's people (v. 4, cf. Rev. 7: 3).   The separating of the innocent from the guilty is in accord with the
principle enunciated in Jer. 31: 29f.; Ezek. 18.   The Hebrew
for mark is *tav*, the same as the last letter of the Hebrew
alphabet, which at that time had a cross shape (either that of
the Latin or St. Andrew's cross).   There can be little doubt
that this is one of the many examples where the Hebrew
prophets spoke better than they knew.

After the killing of the apostates the city itself was set on fire
(10: 2).   Ezekiel's efforts to intercede (9: 8) were of no avail, for
the evil had gone too far.   This is a note frequently struck at
this time, cf. 11: 13; 14: 14; Jer. 7: 16; 11: 14; 14: 11, 15: 1.

"The residue of Israel" is, of course, Judah, the only part of "all Israel" left after the destruction of Samaria.

The Throne of God (10: 3–22)

There is little in the description of the chariot-throne of God here that adds anything to the description already given in 1: 4–28, and it is not clear why the description should be repeated. It may be simply that since Ezekiel will not have preached his call—testimonies were probably not as popular among the prophets as they are with us—the description became a natural and necessary part of his telling of this vision. It was only the later placing in front of it of the story of his call that made this description seem redundant.

Here it is made explicit that the four living creatures, the supporters of the throne, are in fact the cherubim. It is probable that Ezekiel only realized this when he saw them in the temple court and came to understand that they were the beings symbolized by the cherubim in the holy of holies and on the mercy seat. The use of the fire by the angel-scribe (v. 7) is left to our imagination.

There would seem to be considerable textual error in this section, perhaps just because scribes felt that they were dealing with repetition. Verse 14 is the immediate sequel to v. 12; v. 13, referring to the wheels, is out of place—perhaps a scribe's eye was caught by the mention of the wheels at the end of v. 12. There is no suggestion elsewhere that the cherubim (v. 12) were full of eyes; this is said in 1: 18 of the wheels, and it is likely that the text has been disordered. The suggestion of the RSV making v. 12 refer to the wheels is quite possible. Already the rabbis wondered what had happened to the face of an ox in v. 14. Since no explanation is given what the face of a cherub is like, it seems obvious that we have to do with a careless scribal error.

The movements of God in this section are far from clear, and it being a vision, it may be that we should not ask for the coherence that waking sight would give. It is, however, clear that, just as the glory had already left the sanctuary, when Ezekiel first saw it (8: 4) so in 10: 19 it is preparing to leave the temple precincts altogether.

The Judgment on the Priestly Leaders (11: 1–13)

It has been urged that this section is an isolated prophecy, placed here for convenience, or that it has been accidentally moved from its original place after 8: 18; the ground for this view is that there is no room for it here, as God's judgment has already been carried out (9:1–10:2, see especially 9:6) and there is no room for any further judgment.   When, however, the purely symbolic nature of the still future judgment is remembered, the difficulty seems to disappear.   It is, moreover, a commonplace in Hebrew narrative to place elements, which would hold up its flow, out of their strict chronological order.

There are no serious grounds for doubting that the twenty-five men (v. 1) are the same as in 8:16.   The description in v. 6 agrees with 8:17, and their activity in v. 2 suits their position as leading priests, while their blatant idolatry (8:16f.) matches their cynicism (v. 3).   The two names given us cannot be identified with any probability.

With their rejection of Jehovah went a rejection of His will. They refused to see in the capture of Jerusalem and the deportation of Jehoiachin the confirmation of Jeremiah's message and the judgment of God.   They saw in their position a sign of God's favour rather than the reverse.   It is not clear whether we should follow RV tx. or mg. in v. 3, but in either case the general gist of their words is clear enough.   If we take RV tx., it means "Let us prepare for war"; to follow the margin means, "Let us ignore all warnings of judgment to come."   In either case they were basing themselves on the confidence that however hot the flames of Babylonian attack, the city walls would protect them, even as a cauldron protects its contents from the fire.   They were basing themselves on the fact that Nebuchadnezzar had never technically captured Jerusalem (cf. II Kings 24: 12), and still more on their fanatical trust in the temple condemned by Jeremiah (Jer. 7: 4).

"We be the flesh" reflects further the pride of those left in the city, which had already been condemned by Jeremiah (Jer. 24).   For them the exiles under Jehoiachin were the offal thrown out on the dung-heap of Babylonia; they were the good flesh preserved by God in Jerusalem.

The spirit of prophecy fell on Ezekiel (v. 5), and in pronouncing their doom he declared that God's favourites would be those whose deaths they had caused (v. 6f.).   They would not even have the privilege of dying in Jerusalem (v. 7–10). Undoubtedly we have here a prediction of the execution of some of the leaders of the people at Riblah (II Kings 25: 18–21), but since judgment fell on Pelatiah at once, so in the case of some of the others it may have meant merely death in exile.   Death in a heathen land, and that probably without burial, was looked on as an aggravation of God's punishment (cf. Amos 7: 17). A statement like that in v. 7 virtually implies a resurrection, though Ezekiel may not have realized it at the time, for only so could God's value-judgment be openly shown.

Though Pelatiah did not hear Ezekiel's message, there is no ground for considering his death as merely visionary or symbolic. This result of his message was completely unexpected by Ezekiel, and it drove him to intercession (v. 13). Goethe, early in his famous play, shows Faust sitting down to translate the Gospel according to John. He says:

> 'Tis writ, "In the beginning was the word!"
> I pause perplex'd! Who now will help afford?
> I cannot the mere Word so highly prize;
> I must translate it otherwise,
> If by the spirit guided as I read,
> "In the beginning was the Sense!" Take heed,
> The import of this primal sentence weigh,
> Lest thy too hasty pen be led astray!
> Is force creative then of Sense the dower?
> "In the beginning was the Power!"
> Thus should it stand; yet, while the line I trace
> A something warns me, once more to efface.
> The spirit aids! from anxious scruples freed,
> I write, "In the beginning was the Deed!"[1]

Faust here stands for the modern man and his suspicion of words. He has no understanding for the old tales of magic and wonder in which the right word or words are so important. But with all the folly of these tales our forefathers were expressing their awe of words, there having remained with them some broken and distorted memory of the power of the Divine Word.

When Ezekiel spoke the Word of God he had caused something to come into being that was active and creative. The sudden death of Pelatiah reminded him of his other messages of woe, which if allowed to go into full operation, might imperil the existence of all Israel.

The Church today suffers from too much preaching. Sunday by Sunday a spate of words is poured out all around the world, but their fruit is small in proportion to their quantity. Few who speak really grasp that they are there to proclaim the Word of God and not their views about the Word, and so there are only few who know the power that belongs to the Word.

GOD'S GRACE TO THE EXILES (11: 14–21)

God answered Ezekiel's plea by confirming the promise He had earlier given to Jeremiah (Jer. 24) and expanding it. His

[1] Goethe: *Faust*, Pt. I, 1.876–889, translated by A. Swanwick.

promise is apparently addressed not merely to the exiles with
Jehoiachin but also to the earlier exiles from the North ("all of
them," v. 15 RV).   We should follow the chief versions in this
verse and read "the men of thy exile," i.e. thy fellow exiles (so
RSV), instead of the impossible "the men of thy kindred,"
which is not even a true translation of the Hebrew.   We should
also absolve those left in Jerusalem of callous cruelty by rendering with a minor change in the Hebrew vowels "They have
gone far from the LORD" (RSV).   Primitive conceptions like
the one we find in I Sam. 26: 19 were still prevalent; the exiles
were looked on as far from Jehovah, because far from His land,
while those living near the temple were thought to be basking
in the smile of His favour.

The English versions seem to miss the force of the Hebrew in
vv. 16f., which should be rendered: "Whereas I have removed
them . . . and whereas I have scattered them . . . and have become to them a sanctuary in small measure . . . therefore . . . I
will gather you."   In fact v. 16 seems to be an indirect con-
continuation of the Jerusalemites' claim; Jehovah answers it in
v. 17 with a promise of restoration.   The "little sanctuary" of
AV has been a comfort to many, but as a translation it seems to
be linguistically impossible.   We are not dealing with a gracious
promise, but with the spiritual loss felt by the exiles by their
separation from the temple.   The exile was punishment.   Like
all God's punishments it was remedial for some and productive
of ultimate blessing, yet even those that profited most had to
feel its bitterness to the full.

The threefold "you" in v. 17 is emphatic in contrast to v. 15.
The interpretation of v. 19 is complicated by textual difficulties.
Three MSS. and the Syriac read "a new heart and . . . a new
spirit."   The change of text involved in Hebrew is small, but
on the whole it is likely that it is an unconscious or deliberate
assimilation to 18: 31; 36: 26.   LXX and Vulgate read "another
heart and . . . a new spirit."   Here the only change involved
concerns the two most easily confounded letters in Hebrew, R
and D, cf. p. 37.   The present Hebrew text may be supported
by an appeal to Jer. 32: 39, but since here too LXX has in both
cases "another" for "one," we merely have added proof of how
easily these two words could be confused.   The Targum, the
official rabbinic translation into Aramaic, has "a fearful heart."
This is a legitimate paraphrase of either LXX or the Syriac
rendering, but not of the Hebrew.   So we shall probably be
safe in rendering "another heart," or possibly "a new heart,"
there being no essential difference in meaning; the remainder of
the verse seems to support this.   If we retain the Hebrew text,

"one heart" refers presumably to the removal of the old jealousies between north and south, cf. 37: 22. "Within you" should be as in many MSS. and all the versions "within them" (RSV).

Though we shall consider the gracious promise of vv. 17–20 in closer detail, when we deal with its fullest form in 36: 16–38, there is one point that should be noted here. Though Ezekiel stresses the sovereignty of God, he is no determinist. Salvation is God's work, but man has to prepare the way for it by repentance. God brings back the people to their land (v. 17), but before the transformation of character (vv. 19f.), which is also God's work, there is the removal of all traces of idolatry by the people (v. 18), the outward sign of their change of heart. Note in this connexion 18: 31 and see the notes on ch. 18 as a whole.

Similarly the judgment on those left in Jerusalem is nothing arbitrary, the result of an unexplained Divine decree. We have no parallel in the Bible to the expression "the heart of their detestable things" (v. 21). In addition the Hebrew is much more difficult than the English implies. So we should almost certainly make a small emendation and translate with RSV, "But as for those whose heart goes after their detestable things and their abominations . . ." These are in the first place the men of Jerusalem, as the vision of ch. 8 had shown, and their destruction would be the punishment of their impenitent idolatry. But the threat holds good for the exiles too, if they cling to their old idols or turn to the idols of Babylon (cf. 14: 2–6).

THE TEMPLE FORSAKEN (11: 22–25)

Ezekiel's long vision ended with the sight of the withdrawal of the chariot-throne eastward to the Mount of Olives. Years later he was to see it return to the new temple by the way that it had gone (43: 1–4). But from now on, however long the final judgment might be deferred (in fact a trifle under five years), the temple was only an empty shell, and the offerings brought there a mere outward show. Rev. 3: 20 reveals that the same may become true of a Christian church.

CHAPTER VI

WOE TO THE PROPHETS

THE FATE OF KING AND PEOPLE (12: 1–20)

EZEKIEL had told the exiles his vision of the destruction of Jerusalem (11:25). But then he had to reinforce his message by undermining their other sources of self-confidence. The vision of ch. 8–11 was concerned mainly with the temple. Now he turns to the other appointments of God, the king and the prophets. His prophecy about Zedekiah is especially interesting for the enigmatic way in which his fate is foretold, but how literally his actions and words were fulfilled! Note that this prophetic action took place in 591 or 590 B.C. (cf. 20: 1 with 8: 1), but Zedekiah's revolt did not break out till 588 B.C.

The need for the prophecy is given by the term "a rebellious house" applied to the exiles (vv. 2, 3, 9). They were obviously still hoping for an early return to Jerusalem, and so they had no eyes for Ezekiel's vision of destruction. So the prophet revived one of the saddest moments of the exiles' lives by making a little bundle of necessities such as a man would carry as he went into exile and trudging with it over his shoulder to another part of Tel-Abib—"Son of man, prepare for yourself an exile's baggage, and go into exile by day in their sight . . ." (v. 3, RSV, cf. RV mg. to vv. 3, 4). Having awakened the exiles' curiosity, in the evening (v. 4) he carried the bundle home. Before the wondering crowd (v. 5) he dug through the house wall (built of sun-dried bricks, as the poorer houses always were in Babylonia), brought out his bundle, wrapped his face up so that he could not see, and staggered off in the darkness with his bundle.

In the explanation (vv. 10–16) Ezekiel was told that he had acted out the special fate of Zedekiah in the general exile. It looked forward to his flight by night through the breached city wall (II Kings 25: 4), his capture, blinding and leading into exile (II Kings 25: 5ff.). Note that Jehovah is pictured as Himself snaring Zedekiah and bringing him to his doom (v. 13).

In v. 10 we apparently have the same play on the two meanings of *massa'* (cf. RV tx. and mg.) as we have in Jer. 23: 33 (RV mg.). The root meaning of the word is "to lift up," and so it can equally mean a burden, or an oracle lifted up over

the sole definite marks given us by which we may recognize the true prophet are of a nature which demand a truly spiritual man to use them aright.

When Micaiah Ben-Imlah faced Ahab's four hundred prophets (I Kings 22: 19–28), he did not state that they were false prophets, but that Jehovah had deliberately caused them to be led into error. We may reasonably assume that Micaiah considered that normally they were reliable communicators of God's will. A very similar statement is made, as we shall see, by Ezekiel (14: 9f.). The same thought is found in an early prophecy of Jeremiah (4: 10), but here it is not far-fetched to see Jeremiah himself misled for a time by the message of the deceived prophets. Did the false prophets wear a "hairy mantle" (Zech. 13: 4 RV), so did at least Elijah (II Kings 1: 8 RV mg.) and John the Baptist (Matt. 3: 4). Did the "false prophets" do their acted signs, e.g. I Kings 22: 11; Jer. 28: 10, so did at least Isaiah, Jeremiah and Ezekiel. Did the "false prophets" dream dreams and see visions, so did probably all the true prophets as well. When Jeremiah was challenged and contradicted by Hananiah Ben-Azzur (Jer. 28: 1–4), he did not denounce him as a false prophet, he merely maintained that the balance of probability was that he was right and Hananiah was wrong (Jer. 28: 5–9).

Even the apparently clear test of Deut. 18: 22, i.e. the fulfilment of the prophetic message, was not always adequate. Deut. 13: 1f. clearly envisages that the sign given by the prophet might come to pass, even though his object was to seduce the people to follow other gods. In practice it must have been exceptionally difficult to apply this test. That the "false prophets" must very often have been correct in their predictions is obvious enough—however we may explain it— for otherwise they would not have retained public esteem for long. On the other hand the element of contingency in most prophecy made many a prediction of the true prophet *seem* to be falsified. The principle is clearly expressed in Jer. 18: 7–12, and the non-fulfilment of Jonah 3: 4 at the time foretold (though it was fulfilled later) the most obvious example of its application. We shall later find other outstanding examples in Ezekiel's prophecies against Tyre and Egypt, and we may be certain that minor examples were frequent (see especially p. 102). So the remarkable fulfilment of some prophecies—though most of those we consider most remarkable had their fulfilment still future in the earlier part of Ezekiel's prophesying—was offset in the popular mind by the apparent non-fulfilment of others. The strongest influence, however, had been worked by the very long-suffering of God. His postponement of complete doom had been taken to mean that the prophecies of Isaiah and Micah would not go into effect at all (Ezek. 12: 21–28), or at some time in the dim and distant future that did not concern the contemporaries of Jeremiah and Ezekiel, and this in turn prevented the renewed prophecies of doom from being taken very seriously.

The simple fact seems to have been that the "false prophets" could not be classified under any one heading. Some were quite simply mad (cf. Jer. 29: 26); some will have been clever frauds; some were doubtless, to use modern terms, psychic mediums with powers and knowledge more than can be explained by common human experience, whatever may be their source; yet others were godly men who either wished themselves into the body of the prophets instead of awaiting God's call, or having been truly called by God found it easier to compromise with men than to give God's message in all its stark unattractiveness. The last named in particular will have been good and attractive persons whose whole influence seemed placed on God's side, but because it was man's version of God's will that they were proclaiming, they will ultimately have done more harm than the pure deceivers.

We today would for the most part set doctrinal tests for the false prophet, but nothing could be more foolish. Orthodoxy is often nothing more than a sign of spiritual inertia, and the deceiver will always be prepared to say "shibboleth" if he thinks it financially rewarding. In speaking of false prophets the Bible is not concerned with their theological soundness or unsoundness but with their fruits. "By their fruits ye shall know them" said the Lord (Matt. 7: 16), and Jer. 23: 9–40 seems a prophetic commentary on the words. First immorality of life is condemned (vv. 9–14); today too there is far too great a proneness to overlook laxity of living, when a preacher combines orthodoxy in doctrine and great eloquence in preaching. Secondly the prophetic message is condemned which has no bearing on the spiritual needs of the hearers and so reveals that it has not been learnt from God (vv. 15–24). Judged by this standard all too many sermons today fall into the same condemnation. Thirdly the message of unworthy derivation is rejected (vv. 25–29); dreams are not an adequate way in which to learn the message of Almighty God. If some modern preachers were as frank as to the origin of some of their sermons as were the prophets of Israel, we could well pass a similar comment. Then come those that could not even pretend to have received a message from God (vv. 30–32),

but either borrowed it from someone else, or simply invented
something to suit. These shortcomings are not unknown
today also. The problem of the prophet of old was only
the problem of the preacher today in a somewhat different
setting.

This explains why Ezekiel, before he went further with his
message of condemnation, had to try and teach the exiles how
God looked on the prophets whose reiterated message had so
fatally blunted the spiritual receptivity of those that had put
their trust in them.

THE DESPISING OF PROPHECY (12: 21–28)

Quite apart from the effect of the "false prophets," there
were two interrelated obstacles in the minds of his hearers, one
quite general, one linked with Ezekiel himself, that prevented
his message being taken seriously.

The former was one that the exiles had been familiar with
before they had been taken from their homes—"in the land of
Israel" (v. 22); the RSV, though linguistically justifiable,
misses the point—and which was equally current in Jerusalem
and Tel-Abib. It was assumed that because past prophecies of
doom had not gone into fulfilment, they had been annulled, not
merely suspended (v. 22). This attitude of mind can easily be
understood and is reflected in II Pet. 3: 4. Micah and Isaiah
had spoken as though the Assyrian invasions of Judah were the
judgments of the Day of Jehovah instead of their foreshadow-
ing, even as the destruction of Jerusalem in A.D. 70 was a fore-
shadowing of the second coming of Christ in judgment. Instead
of recognizing that the grace of God had caused a postponement
of the worst, they believed that the worst had come and had
proved much easier than expected. In extenuation let us remember that Sennacherib did reduce Judah to a shade of its
former self, so that Hezekiah could venture to use the word
'remnant' (cf. Isaiah's teaching on the remnant) for those that
remained (II Kings 19: 4). When prophets like Huldah (II
Kings 22: 14–17), Zephaniah, Jeremiah and Ezekiel arose, the
bulk of the people just did not take them seriously. Many
doubtless expected punishment for the evil days of Manasseh,
and saw it in the premature death of Josiah and the exile of
Jehoiachin, yet they would not believe that matters could go
any further. Ezekiel assured them that not only his prophecies
but also all the postponed prophecies were about to be fulfilled
(v. 23). In addition all those prophecies of hope that had
falsely buoyed them up (v. 24) would come to an end as well.

The destruction of the temple so discredited the false prophets that they did in fact die out—cf. Zech. 13: 2–6 for a picture of them after the exile.

The second obstacle was one that Ezekiel personally met in the presumably more receptive section of the exiles (vv. 26–28). Their experience had been such as to make them willing to believe his message, but whatever the reason they considered that he was speaking of a future outside their own life-span. To them too came the assurance that all the evils that Ezekiel had foretold were on the verge of fulfilment.

THE FOOLISH PROPHETS (13: 1–16)

This section faces us with several difficulties. One is the surprising fluctuation between the second and the third person. Though we shall not follow out the thought, there is much to be said for the suggestion of ICC *ad loc.* that we have here Ezekiel's interweaving of two prophecies, one in the second person against the prophets in the Babylonian exile (cf. Jer. 29: 8, 15, 21–23, 32), and a second later prophecy against the prophets who had shared in the final fate of Jerusalem. Then there are considerable variations between the Hebrew and the old versions, with the probability that in many cases the versions are correct; certainly the rendering of RSV in vv. 2, 6, 10, 11 is in each case to be preferred.

Ezekiel calls the prophets "foolish"; the word *nabal* is the strongest of the words translated "fool." Where the context calls for it, it means a mental and spiritual obtuseness that borders on atheism; "as applied to the prophets, *nabal* would mean insensible to Jahveh's benefits, as in Deut. 32: 6 (of Israel)" (ICC *ad loc.*). There is no sin in using one's reason; to do so, instead of listening to God, when one is one of God's spokesmen, shows, however, extreme spiritual obtuseness. They prophesied "out of their own heart," i.e. mind (RSV), but they were not just vulgar deceivers. They followed "their own spirit" (v. 3). Spirit (*ruach*) in such a context is something powerful and dominating. Instead of letting themselves be dominated by the Spirit of God, they were dominated by their own desires and motives. It is not the worldly or "unsound" teacher and preacher who is the real danger to the Church, but the man who allows himself so to be dominated by his own deepest desires that he is preaching them, although he has convinced himself that it is the Word of God he is preaching.

Ezekiel compares the prophets to the foxes that live among

ruins (v. 4, RSV),[1] thinking probably mainly of their destruc-
tiveness. In the day of trouble they have neither defended the
"breaches" nor built up the "wall" (v. 5, RSV). They have
had their visions all right (vv. 6, 7), but since they were the
expression of their own desires they were vanity and lies. Self-
deceived they "expect" Jehovah "to fulfil their word" (v. 6,
RSV correctly, cf. RV mg.). When the emptiness of their
message is discovered, they will suffer a threefold punishment
(v. 9): they will lose their honoured place in the councils of the
people, they will be struck out of the citizen-roll of true
Israelites, and they will not return from exile to the land of
Israel again.

One of the main causes of false prophecy is laid bare in vv.
10–16, viz. the instinctive desire to swim with the stream.
Those who denounce traditionalism but for all that are normally its slaves very often fail to realize that only the willingness to put truth before everything else and unflinching surrender of the whole of one's being to the Holy Spirit can keep
a man from proclaiming what he is expected to. The prophets
are pictured as saying, "All is well"—the implication of "Peace"
—and as whitewashing (RSV) the jerrybuilt wall the people
have put up. The very approval (whitewashing) by the
prophets prevented the people seeing how flimsy was their structure until the storm of judgment came and swept it all away.

THE FALSE PROPHETESSES (13: 17–23)

This section is most instructive. Apart from it we know only
of Miriam, Deborah, Huldah and Noadiah as prophetesses, and
the usual tendency has been to regard these four as rare exceptions. But here we see that the prophetess was no uncommon
phenomenon, and it would be unjustified to assume that all,
apart from the four already named, were of the type here
described. It is one more proof of how very dangerous the
argument from silence is, when it is applied to the Bible.

It is clear that the women here described would be termed
sorceresses rather than prophetesses today, and Ezekiel shows
his contempt for them by using the *hithpael* of the verb "to
prophesy" of them in v. 17, rather than the *niphal* he uses elsewhere in the chapter (*ha-mitnabbe'oth* compared with *ha-nib-
ba'im*), a real distinction hardly representable in English.
Seeing, however, that no more doom is pronounced on them
than the complete loss of their influence (v. 23), it is clear that
their sin is less in God's sight than that of the prophets.   Those

[1] Not jackals, as held by many.

who are very fond of quoting I Tim. 2: 11–14 in order to keep
their sisters in Christ in their right place normally overlook that
while the nature of Eve's fall is a reason why the woman should
not be a teacher in the Church, the fact that Adam "was not
deceived" makes his sin the greater, for he sinned open-eyed.
So too in Old Testament times the relatively underprivileged
position of women made them largely the maintainers of the
age-old superstitions of the Near East.   For that little blame
rested on them compared to that incurred by the prophets who
spoke from their own hearts instead of allowing God to speak
through them.

It is only comparatively recently that archaeological research
has made it possible for us to understand the details of the
magic described (for particulars see ICC; there seems no purpose
in discussing them here).   Hence both the AV and RV are de-
fective in their renderings.   In addition the Jews after the
return from exile soon forgot what was intended, and so a
number of scribal errors crept in.   RSV is useful for getting
the correct rendering, though it is probably incorrect in v. 19
along with other English versions.   The handfuls of barley and
crumbs of bread were probably not their pay, but some of their
instruments of divination.   The hunting of souls refers probably to the power that a sorceress will so often gain over those
that consult her.

A passage like this is a needed reminder how far short popular
religion fell of the teaching of the prophets.   It should be clear
too that those that resorted to magic arts and divination would
not be likely to have an ear for the spiritual message of the
prophets.

THE IDOLATER AND THE PROPHET (14: 1–11)

Before Ezekiel can leave the "false prophets," there is yet
another aspect of the problem to be dealt with.   A generation
normally had the prophets it wanted, just as a church normally
has the ministry it secretly wants.   So here we have a picture
of the men who were largely responsible for the flourishing of
the "false prophets."

They are called "elders of Israel" (cf. 20: 1); it is not likely
that any difference between them and "the elders of Judah"
(8: 1) is intended.   They are said to "have taken their idols
into their heart," which probably means that they had set their
affections on them.   They are spoken of as typifying the people
generally (vv. 4, 7), and so there is no reason for inferring that
they were particularly guilty themselves.   On the other hand,

since apart from this passage there is no evidence for idolatry among the exiles, it may well be that Ezekiel is referring not merely to the visible forms of idolatry as described in ch. 8 but also and with equal stress to all the false gods of the heart that separate a man's allegiance from Jehovah.

No greater insult can be offered to God than for the man who offers Him no allegiance, or at best a divided one, which He will not accept, to come to His prophet and to ask to know His will, which he will only do, if it suits him.   He may do it to seem respectable in the eyes of man, or out of superstition, or just because it is customary.   In any case, the prophet will be silent and "I the Lord will answer him Myself" (RSV, vv. 4 (!), 7). The answer will be one of such judgment that it will "seize the house of Israel by their heart" (v. 5, ICC).   The prophet will be silent, not because he has seen through the man's hypocrisy, but because God has given him no answer, and the true prophet does not speak unless he has a word from God.   This does not exclude the possibility of the man's doom being declared by the prophet.

What of the false prophet?   The true prophet, who looked only to God, could afford to be silent, but not so the false prophet.   His reputation depended on his being able to give an acceptable answer, whenever it was wanted.   Faced by the Divine silence, when the idolater asked Jehovah's will, he would be enticed (v. 9, RV mg.) and give the type of answer that would give most satisfaction.   All unknown to him, however, God would be behind the answer, using it to the destruction of both the enquirer and the prophet.   The false prophet does not create a generation that does not know God, but is created by it, and he is one of God's instruments of judgment on that generation.

The Absolute Justice of Jerusalem's Punishment
(14: 12–23)

Before passing on to a long series of oracles foretelling and motivating the doom of Jerusalem and of the royal house, Ezekiel had first to deal with any false hopes that might weaken the effect of his message.   We have already seen how he dealt with the optimistic oracles of the false prophets.   There yet remained that last hope that springs eternal in the human breast, the hope that somehow, it might be out of the kindness of God's heart, it might be because of one's link with some godly man, God might make some form of exception in one's favour. It is this hope that Ezekiel now demolishes.

To appreciate the full weight of the oracle we must remind ourselves how Ezekiel had already stressed the evil of Jerusalem, especially in the long vision 8: 1–11: 25, and how he had made clear that the future of the nation lay with the exiles under Jehoiachin (11: 14–20). But some may have snatched at the mention of those that bore God's mark (9: 4) and have said that they at least might involve others in their own safety. God's blunt answer is that, if they were even the most righteous of men, they could not do this.

No entirely satisfactory reason has ever been given why precisely Noah, Daniel and Job are mentioned. ICC (p. 153) says, "The prophet names three typically righteous men, who, on account of their righteousness, were enabled to achieve a work of deliverance: Noah delivered his family, Gen. 6: 8; 7: 1; Daniel his companions, Dan. 1: 6–20; Job his friends, Job 42: 7–10; but the righteousness of all three together could not deliver the present generation." While true enough of Noah, it hardly carries conviction for Job and Daniel. Furthermore, it must be looked on as extremely doubtful whether the well-known Daniel is intended at all. His name, as indeed that of the other two Daniels of Scripture, was spelled *Daniyye'l*, but Ezekiel spells it *Dani'el*, or more likely *Dan'el*. He would seem to be referring to a figure of hoar antiquity probably mentioned in tablets discovered at Ras Shamra dating from before 1400 B.C. A scribal error on Ezekiel's part is most unlikely. If so, we know too little to form any opinion as to why he was mentioned.

On the other hand it should be noted that Job's righteousness was not able to save even his own property and family, and Noah only saved those animals and persons expressly designated by God. So it seems more likely that Ezekiel is stressing not the little they had been able to save, but that they had not been able to save. This would explain why Abraham, who would be far more suitable on the ordinary view, is in fact not named, or for that matter Moses.

The fact that God is bringing on Jerusalem all four—four with the suggestion of completeness—of His major scourges (v. 21) shows the greatness of Jerusalem's sin and the resultant hopelessness that any should escape, except those few marked by God (9: 4). "Yet, if there should be left in it any survivors to lead out sons and daughters" (v. 22 RSV; AV and RV have missed the point), it would be purely for the sake of the exiles in Babylonia, not for the good of those that escape.

Ezekiel works out the principle underlying this oracle in more detail in ch. 18. Here it will suffice to point out that God's judgments are not on actions as such, but on actions as indicative of character. I may do another's stint of duty as well as my own, but I do not change his character by so doing. Behind Abraham's pleading for Sodom and Gomorrah (Gen. 18) lay the hope that the righteous might yet turn the wicked from their way. When he stopped at ten righteous, it was not from lack of faith in God's mercy, but from his keen understanding that if Lot had not been able to exercise that much influence, there was no hope that he would ever be able to turn the Cities of the Plain from their evil ways. He who does not let himself be influenced by the righteous, cannot expect to be able to profit from the "merits" of the righteous in the day of judgment.

THE PARABLE OF THE VINE (15: 1–8)

The comparison of Israel to a vine was an old one, probably as early as Gen. 49: 22 (so most modern commentaries), but it was normally used to stress the lack of the fruit desired by God, cf. Deut. 32: 32; Hos. 10: 1; Isa. 5: 1–7; Jer. 2: 21. Ezekiel takes this reiterated picture for granted and compares not the cultivated vine of the vineyard, but the wild vine in the forest (i.e. Israel merely as a nation among nations) with other trees and asks what superiority it has (v. 2). The answer is that it obviously has none, but that it is rather inferior in every respect (v. 3). Now, however, that Israel had been charred (RSV) at both ends and in the middle by the exile of Jehoiachin and his companions (v. 4) it was completely useless (v. 5) and there only remained for what was left to be burned up (v. 6f.). In other words the deportation of Jehoiachin had shown that the time for fruit-bearing was finally past, and therefore only the logical fate of destruction remained for those that were left.

CHAPTER VII

JERUSALEM, QUEEN AND HARLOT

AN ALLEGORY OF JERUSALEM (16: 1–63)

THIS is, with the probable exception of ch. 40–48, Ezekiel's most elaborate allegory. The fact that it ill accords with modern taste is no ground for passing over it quickly, for it stresses some of his basic concepts. It may be too that, if we had not developed a false modesty, we should not have so much pernicious sexual description in many a modern novel. Of course the imagery is ugly and unattractive, but it only matches the even more ugly sin it represents.

The chapter falls naturally into four divisions, vv. 1–43, 44–52, 53–59 and 60–63. There is every reason for thinking that the first and second divisions represent distinct but related oracles, while for reasons given in their right place the last two divisions are probably later than the destruction of Jerusalem.

The use of Jerusalem is purely symbolic. It has no reference to the city as such, but to the southern kingdom, which in the first division, as is usually the case in Ezekiel, represents all Israel. No reference of any kind is intended to the pre-Israelite past of the city. Many would see in "the Amorite was thy father, and thy mother was a Hittite" (vv. 3, 45) a historic note about the origin of Jerusalem,[1] but it is extremely improbable that this is meant especially in the light of v. 45. It is far more likely that the Amalekite and the Hittite stand for the Semitic and non-Semitic elements that made up the Canaanite scene during the period of the Patriarchs and at the Conquest.

THE FOUNDLING CHILD GOD'S BRIDE (16: 1–14)

Ezekiel is far too skilful an artist to make the common mistake of those that deal in allegories. He makes no effort to make the *details* of his story tie up with the details of the Patriarchal period. He is concerned to give a general spiritual picture, not the outward historical one. Two things are stressed, the foundling's completely weak and unwanted position, and her positive and negative ignorance of God.

The former is stressed in vv. 4–6. The careful reader of the

[1] E.g. F. F. Bruce: *The Hittites.*

Patriarchal stories may well notice an apparent inner contradiction running through them, a contradiction which has been
used by many modern scholars to strengthen their theories that
we need attribute little historical value to them.   Sometimes
the Patriarchs seem to be rich and powerful, sometimes they
seem weak and relatively poor.   Though we are not yet able to
give a certain explanation, the discoveries of recent archaeology
suggest that it may well lie in the conditions of the time, one of
great folk-movements that wrought great changes on the face
of the Near East.

Now in Gen. 14: 13 we find the title "the Hebrew" attached
to the name Abram.   Two meanings for it have normally been
offered, either "descendant of Eber" (cf. Gen. 10: 24f.), or "the
man from the other side," i.e. "the immigrant," but neither
interpretation is supported by the other uses of "Hebrew," or
by the apparently cognate forms discovered by archaeology.
An example is its use in Gen. 40: 15, for it is impossible to sup-
pose that the descendants of Abraham had grown so powerful
in Canaan, or one of its districts, that it had become known to
the Egyptians as their land.   Equally a different sense seems
demanded in Gen. 43: 32.   The concordance will show that
Hebrew is not Israel's name for itself.

Archaeology has established an almost certain link between
Hebrew and the Habiru (Akkadian), Apiru (Egyptian) and 'prm
(Ras Shamra; vowels uncertain), who are found in inscriptions
ranging from the nineteenth to the twelfth centuries B.C.   It is
obviously not a national name; they are "landless soldiers,
raiders, captives and slaves of miscellaneous ethnic origins."[1]
Some form of poverty, landlessness or lower social standing
seems implicit in the name, whatever its actual meaning may
be, and so we can best understand it in Ex. 21: 2; Deut. 15: 12;
Jer. 34: 9, 14.

If then we bear in mind the almost certain social stigma
implied in "Abram the Hebrew" and that, as the story of
Joseph shows, the name clung to his descendants, and if we add
the degradation of the slavery in Egypt that followed, it becomes very much easier to understand Ezekiel's very strong
picture in vv. 4–6.

Far worse, however, is the ignorance of God implied.   Whatever the precise implication of "I throughly washed away thy
blood from thee" (v. 9), we cannot reasonably disassociate it
from v. 6, which is best rendered "In thy blood live" (ICC).
The pollution of Israel's birth remained until the time of
Jehovah's marriage with her (vv. 8–10), viz., at Sinai.   However

[1] W. F. Albright: *From the Stone Age to Christianity*, p. 182.

high the faith of the leading patriarchs, the beliefs of Abraham's old home had lived on among the people until at least the time of Joshua (Josh. 24: 14f.). We have it also implied in Gen. 35: 2, for the action there described was of course merely external, and in the story of the golden calf (Ex. 32), which is best explained by Semitic and not by Egyptian parallels. We have no grounds for thinking Gen. 38: 1–6 to be in any way exceptional, and it is a fair supposition that virtually all Jacob's daughters-in-law were drawn from heathen stock, thus largely explaining v. 3. Then 23: 3 makes explicit what is here implicit, that Egypt strengthened the root of heathenism in Israel. This is also implied by v. 7 rightly understood. The Hebrew, "I made thee a myriad" (AV mg., RV mg.), obviously contradicts the allegory, and the same is true of the AV and RV text. We should render with LXX and Syriac, "Grow up like a plant of the field" (RSV). In other words the foundling was left to grow up a young savage, by the light of nature, naked! This is probably the main reason why Moses and not Abraham is always looked back to as the founder of Israel's religion.

The "badgers' skin" (v. 10—RV "sealskin") should be simply "leather" (RSV) and so also in Ex. 25: 5, etc.

The Harlot (16: 15–34)

This section covers the spiritual history of the people from the Conquest to the prophet's own time. He speaks of a harlot, and of whoredom or fornication rather than of adultery and of an adulteress, for it is not so much the disloyalty of Israel that is being stressed, as so often, but rather her unnatural and irresponsible wantonness. The adulteress may by some be excused by the strength of passion and blind love, but for a harlot there is no excuse except that of stark necessity. But for Israel there is not even this excuse. She has not been paid by her lovers, but has paid those that have taken their pleasure of her (vv. 31, 33f.).

The first stage in the downward path is in vv. 15–22. Here the amalgamation of Jehovah worship with the religion of the Canaanites, which was the besetting religious sin of Israel, is described (see p. 36, or in more detail my *Men Spake from God*, p. 36f.). This religion, though considered Jehovah worship by the people, was point-blank called Baal worship by the prophets without the least qualification. Its climax was human sacrifice (vv. 20f.). There are no reasons for thinking that it was practised after the period of the Judges (and then only exceptionally,

Judges 11: 31, 39) until the times of Ahaz and Manasseh (II Kings 16: 3; 21: 6, Mic. 6: 7). But it was always the logical conclusion of bringing Jehovah down to the level of a nature god, for as Jer. 7: 31 makes quite clear, it was to Jehovah that these sacrifices were offered. *Molech* (II Kings 23: 10) is only Jehovah's title as king (*melech*) with the rabbinically added vowels of *bosheth* (shame).

The second stage of the downward path is given in vv. 23–34, that of open apostasy and idolatry, again a natural consequence of debased religion. The meaning of v. 24 is far from certain. The Greek, Syriac and Latin versions all understood a reference to brothels and their signs, and it is quite likely that Ezekiel is referring to the high places in this way. Since, specially in the northern kingdom, they were centres of immorality in the name of religion, the picture would be apposite.

The truly allegorical nature of Ezekiel's oracle may be seen in his reference to Egypt. So far as we can judge, Egyptian religion, apart from the cult of Isis, who came to be identified with Ashtoreth or Astarte, was seldom exported and we have no direct Biblical record of the worship of Egyptian gods, not even in I Kings 11: 4–8, where it might have been expected (cf. also p. 42). The worship referred to in v. 26 was the constant turning to Egypt for help against Assyria, a practice so strongly condemned by Hosea and Isaiah. To look to Egypt for help implied a recognition of the power of Egypt's gods, even though they might receive no formal worship. Ezekiel's epithet "great of flesh" applied to Egypt (cf. 23: 19–21) shows partly Ezekiel's deep repugnance for all things Egyptian, partly the bitter lesson that Israel was so slow to learn from experience that the apparent strength of Egypt was only flabby fat.

The only effect of turning to Egypt in the time of Hezekiah had been the cutting short of Judean territory by Sennacherib, who handed over many of the cities he had captured to the Philistine kings who had remained loyal to him.[1]

Ezekiel then passes over to Assyria (v. 28) and Chaldea, i.e. Babylonia named after the ruling people in it (v. 29). For the latter before the rise of Babylon to world power see II Kings 20: 12–19. The sense has been missed in v. 29; we should render "with the trading land of Chaldea" (RSV, cf. RV mg.). The Canaanites, particularly in their Phoenician branch, were great traders, and so "Canaan," "Canaanite" are used in the sense of trade and trader, e.g. 17: 4; Hos. 12: 7; Zeph. 1: 11; Zech. 14: 21; Prov. 31: 24, cf. RV tx. and mg. in each case. In the case of Assyria the recognition of the power of its gods was

[1] See Pritchard: *Ancient Near Eastern Texts*, p. 288a.

actively expressed by the worship of "the host of heaven" from the time of Ahaz and Manasseh to Josiah's reformation.

It should be specially noticed that he makes not the slightest mention of the many attempts at reformation in the history of Israel. One and all they had been external for all but a handful of people, and the heart of the people had remained unchanged, even if the outward forms of worship had been altered. It has been one of the worst features of the traditional exegesis of the Old Testament that it has normally ignored the plain teaching of Ezekiel and of other prophets and has tried to whitewash many of the Old Testament characters and has deliberately placed many incidents in far too favourable a light.

The Judgment on the Harlot (16: 35–43)

Provided we do not try unduly to stress the allegory the main picture is correct. It was the unfaithfulness of Jehoiakim and Zedekiah (see especially 17: 13f., 16) that led to Nebuchadnezzar's destruction of Jerusalem. Though obviously there was no joining together as such of her lovers (v. 37) to destroy her, yet Israel had been progressively weakened by all the peoples she had come into contact with, when she was unfaithful to Jehovah, and in this way they had prepared her for her final doom.

The Allegory of the Sisters (16: 44–52)

A new allegory begins with v. 44, but though it is not the continuation of the preceding one, it is obviously closely linked with it in thought, and no doubt in time too. In the former, Jerusalem, though strictly symbolizing only Judah, obviously refers to the history of Israel as a whole. In the latter Jerusalem stands for the Southern Kingdom only, while Samaria represents the Northern. But what of Sodom?

Sodom is depicted as dwelling "at thy right hand" (v. 46), i.e. south of Jerusalem. The cities of the Plain probably lay at the north end of the Dead Sea;[1] i.e. due east of Jerusalem; but since this is an allegory, and Sodom is pictured as balancing Samaria to the north—"at thy left hand"—this is not sufficient evidence on which to hold that a literal Sodom is not intended. But even though "elder" and "younger" (v. 46) mean more and less powerful than Jerusalem (Samaria was a very recent city compared to Jerusalem; I Kings 16: 24), it is hardly likely that Ezekiel is joining together two capitals and a mere provincial

[1] For a different view see *The Westminster Historical Atlas to the Bible*, p. 65f.

E

town.   In addition we must remember that there is no parallel
in Scripture to the promise of the restoration of Sodom in vv.
53, 55.   Since the promise to Samaria and Jerusalem in v. 53
is obviously literal, we have no right to spiritualize that to
Sodom.   Furthermore it is not a restoration of cities that is
meant, but of their rightful inhabitants.   Samaria had never
ceased to be a city.   Sargon immediately after its capture claims,
"The town I rebuilt better than it was before and settled therein
people from countries which I myself had conquered."[1]   So it
seems reasonable, remembering that this is an allegory, and
that there were no Sodomites to restore, to see in Sodom the
small heathen states and cities left round Israel.   Since the
essential link of the Israelite kingdoms with Canaan is stressed
(v. 45), there seem to be no valid grounds for not seeing in
Sodom all that had survived of the Canaanites and their
culture.   After all, most had been smashed by Sennacherib
and the remnant were to share in the coming destruction,
cf. ch. 25.

The "daughters" of the three sisters are presumably, as so
often, the dependent towns and villages of the main cities.

It is impossible to set out in mathematical terms wherein
Jerusalem's sin was greater than that of her sisters.   God's
standard of judgment takes factors into consideration which can
only tentatively be used by men.   Sodom's sin was not unnatural, as was that of the harlot Jerusalem; it was the working
out of the inherent weakness of Canaanite religion.   It should
not be forgotten, and it is of outstanding importance for the
interpretation of this allegory, that the destruction of Sodom
by God was only the first act in His judgment on Canaan that
should have been completed by the Israelites at the conquest,
but which was in fact carried out very half-heartedly.   Israel
knew that the religion of Canaan was under the judgment of
God, so all copying of it made them more guilty than those
whom they copied.

It is doubtless true that the Northern Kingdom never showed
such religious corruption as did Judah in the reign of Manasseh,
but it is not here that we have to seek the greater sin of Jerusalem as compared with Samaria.   It is rather that Judah
refused to learn the lesson of the downfall of the Northern
Kingdom (23: 11; Jer. 3: 6–13).

If I am right in holding that vv. 53–59 are a later addition
(see below), then the lesson of this allegory is that since Sodom
and Samaria rightly went to their doom, there can be no hope
at all for Jerusalem, for her sins are even blacker.

[1] See Pritchard: *Ancient Near Eastern Texts*, p. 284b.

The Restoration of the Sisters (16: 53–59)

There are two reasons why we should look on these verses as Ezekiel's later ending to his allegory. The shame he foretells for Jerusalem, which is the main point here, would turn away the hearers' thought from the original lesson of the allegory, which was the certain destruction of Jerusalem. In addition, and more important, until judgment has fallen on Jerusalem, Ezekiel holds out hope for the exiles brought to Babylonia with Jehoiachin, but not for the doomed city. It would be quite inconsistent with the ever darkening gloom of his oracles to give even this qualified word of hope.

All prophecy is contingent (Jer. 18: 7–10, cf. p. 102), and so the promise of restoration to Sodom and Samaria is conditional on their repentance, even though that is not mentioned. But though, largely thanks to the work of Ezekiel, Judah was restored and Israel was not, except in so far as it amalgamated with Judah (cf. p. 132), the prophecy had a remarkable fulfilment. It was not until the second century B.C. under the Hashmoneans that Jerusalem began to win back something of its old splendour. For long it was outshone by Samaria and other cities of the land.

Reconciliation (16: 60–63)

Here in these verses we have both the conclusion of the allegory of the unfaithful wife and of that of the sisters. It is also to be dated after the fall of Jerusalem for the same reasons as vv. 53–59. The marriage had been broken beyond hope of repair (Jer. 3: 1, RV mg.) and the full punishment of God had to fall on the sinful people. But, for all that, God would in free grace once again pick them up, once again make a covenant with them, once again take them as His bride. The details of the promise must wait until we come to ch. 36, where they are developed in full, but for the present let us remember Jeremiah's great promise, which lies behind Ezekiel's message: "Behold the days come, saith Jehovah, that I will make a new covenant with the house of Israel and with the house of Judah; not according to the covenant that I made with their fathers . . . forasmuch as they brake My covenant, and I had to lord it over them . . . I will put My law in their inward parts, and in their heart will I write it; and I will be their God, and they shall be My people . . . I will forgive their iniquity, and their sin will I remember no more" (Jer. 31: 31–34).

In the light of such an act of grace Jerusalem can be restored

to her pre-eminence once more, but there is ever to remain the
memory of the path of shame she had trodden. God would
blot out the past, but the very memory of it would keep Jerusalem faithful to Him.

THE TREACHEROUS FOLLY OF ZEDEKIAH (17: 1–24)

This chapter is a prophecy of Zedekiah's doom, not of his
actions. We may, therefore, reasonably date it about 588 B.C.,
the time of Zedekiah's revolt against Nebuchadnezzar. This
would place it later than 20:1, which is dated in 590 B.C.
There is little doubt that the break in chronological order is
deliberate, for ch. 17 is a necessary appendix to ch. 16.

The coming judgment on Jerusalem was to be a judgment on
the whole history of Israel, yet it was a judgment on its last
generation as well. Their repentance could have postponed the
day of doom, as did the reformations of Hezekiah and Josiah,
though it could not have permanently averted it. So Ezekiel
turns from the long story of Israel's apostasy (ch. 16) to the
criminal and sacrilegious folly of those left in Jerusalem.

His message is in "a riddle and . . . a parable" (RSV "allegory"). At the same time the riddle is so transparent, that it
would have been a thick head indeed that did not understand
it. The reason for the form of the message is not far to seek.
The hearts of the majority of the exiles will always have been
with those that prophesied an early return (cf. p. 16). They
had been discredited, but with the outbreak of Zedekiah's
rebellion the hopes of many must have flared up again, and
Ezekiel's message of doom will have grown increasingly unpopular. So he tried yet another method to gain his hearers'
attention.

The actual language of the allegory needs little comment.
The imagery used may seem bizarre to us, but its individual
portions are found elsewhere in the Bible. The eagle, or rather
vulture, quite apart from being the largest bird of the Near
East, is symbolic of the speed of the conqueror (Jer. 48:40;
49: 22; Isa. 46: 11); for the cedar representing the Davidic
house one may compare Isa. 10: 33 – 11: 1. Most commentators
satisfy themselves with the remark that the metaphor is changed
in v. 5, but that is surely to deal superficially with such a master
of the symbolic as Ezekiel. In dealing with 12: 12 (p. 51) we
saw that Ezekiel did not regard Zedekiah, but Jehoiachin as
the true king. Similarly in 11: 14–21 (cf. Jer. 24) it is made
abundantly clear that the true Israel was to be sought for in
captivity, not among those left in the land. So the change

from the cedar to the vine shoot carries its own implied condemnation with it, especially in the light of ch. 15.   Further
evidence that the change of metaphor has this deeper meaning
is seen in the derogatory "seed of the land" (v. 5); this does
indeed stress the generosity of Nebuchadnezzar in not putting
a foreign ruler over the land, but it is not a natural expression
for a member of the royal family.   We should note too the
return to the picture of the cedar in vv. 22ff., when Ezekiel deals
with the true king who is to come.

Ezekiel condemns first of all the folly of Zedekiah's action.
Though the first eagle had planted the vine shoot "beside many
waters," it turned to the second eagle to be watered!   Judah
had been so reduced in strength that all it could hope for by a
successful rebellion against Babylon was a change of masters,
and Egypt, being nearer, would probably have made its hand
felt the more heavily.

More important was the breach of Zedekiah's oath (v. 13,
II Chron. 36: 13).   We do not know enough of the circumstances to understand Ezekiel's stress on this.   Presumably in
all cases where kings of Israel or Judah had voluntarily or under
duress accepted the overlordship of Assyria they had sworn an
oath of loyalty.   Evidently there were special circumstances
operating in Zedekiah's case; that Nebuchadnezzar himself felt
bitterly about it is suggested by his exemplary punishment of
Zedekiah (II Kings 25:6f.).   Ezekiel says that since Zedekiah
had called Jehovah as witness to his oath ("Mine oath . . . My
covenant," v. 19), Jehovah would guarantee Nebuchadnezzar's
victory and Zedekiah's punishment.

Finally Ezekiel confirms his stress that not in Jerusalem and
its present ruler is the hope of the future to be found.   The
deliberately enigmatic language of vv. 22ff. without any explanation is probably to be explained by his knowledge of Jer.
22: 28ff.   He does not want to increase the anguish of the king
in exile by an express reference to the doom already uttered,
but for the careful hearer the implication was there.   It was
not the transplanted cedar twig that was to be re-planted "in
the mountain of the height of Israel," i.e. Zion, but another
twig altogether, not taken from the twig growing in exile, but
from the parent tree.   But there had to be a re-planting, which
implied that the old dynastic tree had in fact met its doom, cf.
Isa. 11: 1, where stem (AV), stock (RV) are best rendered
stump (RSV).   "All the trees of the field" (v. 24), means all
the mighty of the world; for the thought of the verse cf. both
the song of Hannah (I Sam. 2: 1–10) and the song of Mary
(Luke 1: 46–55).   (Many take the passage as a promise to

Jehoiachin's descendants, but I believe this to rest on an insufficiently careful reading of vv. 3f., 22.)

There is no need to doubt the Messianic nature of the passage, though this is not stressed. Both Jeremiah and Ezekiel knew that the Messianic hope was one of the causes why the people did not take the warnings of doom sufficiently seriously. So neither of them was prepared to stress the hope until the doom had come.

If the passage is Messianic, then the beasts (LXX, RSV) and the birds must represent the nations of the world that come to the Messianic king (cf. Isa. 2: 2ff.). This being so, we would do well not to accept without due thought the interpretation of the Parable of the Mustard Seed (Mark 4: 30–32) which demands that the birds that come and lodge in the branches of the mustard plant must of necessity be symbols of something evil.[1]

[1] This view has recently found eloquent re-affirmation in Lang: *Pictures and Parables*, pp. 87–92.

CHAPTER VIII

GOD AND THE INDIVIDUAL

THE INDIVIDUAL AND THE JUSTICE OF GOD (18: 1–32)

FOR those who insist on regarding the prophets as inspired dogmatic theologians with the added gift of being able to see the future this chapter and 33: 1–20 create very real difficulties. They are in apparent contradiction with so much in Ezekiel and also apparently over-simplify human experience. Further they seem to deny the doctrine of the perseverance of the saints and to present a legalistic conception of salvation without parallel in the Bible. If on the other hand we are prepared to accept the prophets as being first and foremost God's spokesmen to their own generation and dealing with the problems of their own times, most of the difficulties vanish.

The subordination of the individual to the community in the Old Testament, though a fact, is normally exaggerated. The Divine principle of justice, "visiting the iniquity of the fathers upon the children" (Ex. 20: 5; 34: 7; Deut. 5: 9) is *never* carried over into Israelite law. The suggestion by some critics that Deut. 24: 16 shows the influence of a later and better period has no evidence to support it, for nothing can be based on the acts of a man like Ahab (II Kings 9: 26). There are only two apparent exceptions to this statement. But in the punishment of Saul's sons and grandsons for the wrong done to the Gibeonites (II Sam. 21: 1–9) it is not primarily a wrong done to men that is being punished, but the breach of a solemn oath (Joshua 9: 15, 19). When we consider Achan's fate more closely, it should be obvious that the fact that even his inanimate household goods share in it (Joshua 7: 24ff.) shows that the true explanation is, that by bringing the stolen articles into his tent, he had made it and his family and his goods an extension of Jericho that had to share the fate of Jericho. For that matter the killing of Naboth's sons may have been "justified" by their father's having been condemned for blasphemy (I Kings 21: 10, 13).

In other words, if the children suffered with their parents, the innocent with the guilty, it was God's doing. But even then "visiting the iniquity of the fathers upon the children upon the third and upon the fourth generation of them that hate Me" is far outweighed by "shewing mercy (steadfast love, RSV) unto a thousand generations (RV mg., AJV) of them that love Me." In addition the fact that the fundamental laws of the Pentateuch are always addressed to the individual shows that the responsibility for their observance must always be in the first place individual.

The fact is that the popular modern conception of the individual is derived from Greek thought rather than from the Bible, and may even be regarded as anti-Biblical. We tend to think of our bodies giving us our individuality and separating us, one from the other. In the Old Testament it is our flesh—a word for body hardly exists in Hebrew—that binds us to our fellow-men; it is our personal responsibility to God that gives us our individuality. Since man (*'adam*) is bound to the ground (*'adamah*) from which he has been taken, and through it to all who live on the same ground, he cannot help influencing them by his actions. Abominable conduct causes "the land to sin" (Deut. 24: 4; cf. Jer. 3: 1, 9). That is why drought, pestilence, earthquake, etc., are for the Old Testament the entirely natural punishment of wickedness (cf. Psa. 107: 33f.). If a man dwelt in a polluted land, he could not help sharing in its pollution. The chief terror of exile was not that the land of exile was outside the control of Jehovah—a view that was probably held by very few—but rather that it was an unclean land (Amos 7: 17).

The repetition of the main message of this chapter in 33: 10–20, where Ezekiel is re-commissioned for his work after the fall of Jerusalem, a repetition which in its literary form must be due to the prophet himself, gives the vital clue to its interpretation. It is fundamentally a message to the exiles, not to those that had been left in Jerusalem. For the latter Ezekiel had no message except of doom—and it is worth noticing that, if we confine ourselves to his prophecies spoken after the deportation of Jehoiachin, this is true of Jeremiah too. But even of them Ezekiel makes it clear that the *few* righteous among them would be delivered (9: 4; 14: 14). There is no Old Testament passage that suggests that the righteous must perish with the wicked, but they will suffer with them.

"In the land of Israel" (v. 2, RV mg.) among the survivors a mood of deep pessimism had crept in. The prophets' message of doom had produced the attitude that, if the people were doomed through the sins of their ancestors, it was no use for them, "the children" (v. 2), to bother about their own behaviour. They assumed that the effect of their ancestors' guilt

would outweigh the rare righteousness of their descendants.
Jeremiah answered this attitude (Jer. 31: 29f.) by proclaiming
a revelation of the grace of God in a new covenant that could
break the whole entail of the past (Jer. 31: 31–34).

Cynical and pessimistic "wisecracks" travel fast, and the
proverb had reached the exiles, who used it in rather a different
sense. They implied by it that Jeremiah and Ezekiel were at
fault in proclaiming that the exile was God's grace to them. If
that were so, they would prosper, but as it was, "Our trans-
gressions and sins are upon us, and we pine away in them; how
then should we live?" (33: 10). For men with no knowledge
or hope of true life after death the only certain sign of God's
favour they knew was earthly prosperity; without it they were
obviously under the wrath of God—the whole theme of *Job*
revolves around this concept.

Ezekiel does not deny corporate suffering, which affects the
righteous also. In 11: 14–21 he had made it clear that exile
was a place of suffering and deprivation, though ultimately of
spiritual blessing (see p. 47), a theme expanded in 36: 22–36.
But whereas in a few short years a doom would descend on
Jerusalem that would leave only a handful of survivors (14:
12–23), the exiles would *live*. Obviously Ezekiel is not thinking
of eternal life and death in the Christian sense, but of physical
survival, when so many were to go down to Sheol. A study of
the later chapters of his prophecy shows that he had a deeper
meaning as well. Like so many others among the prophets the
future was foreshortened for him, and he hoped that the restoration that he foretold would follow immediately on the sufferings
of his own time. In other words, those who lived might live on
into the Messianic age in which death was to be abolished (Isa.
25: 6ff.). So in fact he was speaking better than he knew, for
those who lived in Ezekiel's sense will surely be sharers of fuller
life at the resurrection.

Since God had brought the exiles to Babylonia for a spiritual
purpose, it was obvious that He had to make spiritual men and
women of them. Those who showed by their lives that they
belonged spiritually to those that had remained in Jerusalem,
or who decided that it was not worth paying the price to obtain
the promises proclaimed by Ezekiel would of necessity have to
be weeded out of His remnant by God. Under normal conditions God might use prosperity and sufferings as His judgments. In the misery of exile, however, where most were
stripped to the minimum of life, life and death became the
criteria of God's attitude. This explains why ch. 18 is so
phrased in black and white.

RIGHTEOUSNESS AND WICKEDNESS

The Bible exists to give God's judgment of man, not that man may sit in judgment on his fellow-man. So it normally pictures the extremes, leaving him who is neither one thing nor the other to the judgment of his God, who is the reader of all his secrets and motives. Here the contrast is drawn between the just (RSV "righteous," *tsaddiq*) and the wicked (*rasha'*).

The *tsaddiq* is the man who lives up to a standard; in the Bible obviously God's standard. In the Old Testament that standard is the Law, and the test of living is mainly an external one. But we should never make the mistake of labelling the Old Testament as legalistic. The *tsaddiq* knew that he had not achieved the standard perfectly, and that if God accepted him, it was in grace. But on the other hand his actions were the ground of his acceptance because they revealed the true desires of his heart. The *rasha'* is the man who deliberately rejects God's Law, in part or whole. To men he may sometimes seem attractive, but he is rejected by God, because his actions show his true attitude towards God.

The test of character given by Ezekiel is instructive. The list begins with the centuries' old sin of Israel, the Canaanized, idolatrous worship of Jehovah (v. 6a). Then follows sexual passion which respects neither one's neighbour's home nor the normal decencies of married life (v. 6b). Next we have the taking advantage of another's weakness, either by ignoring the law to which he dare not appeal, or by open robbery (RSV) (v. 7a). Next in order come simple inhumanity and hardness of heart (v. 7b). Then v. 8 condemns the man who profits from his riches, from his neighbour's weakness of character, or from his position in society, while v. 9 presents the demands of the law in a generalized way.

It will be seen that the picture often given of Ezekiel as a formalist finds no support here. He, as do all the prophets, proclaims man's attitude to his fellow-man as the true index of his attitude towards God. The mention of idolatrous worship in the first place is no denial of this. The peculiar evil of the Canaanized worship of Jehovah, condemned by the prophets as Baal worship, lay in its reducing Jehovah to the level of a nature god, whose demands consequently were largely ritual and mostly arbitrary rather than moral.[1]

It is worth stressing once again that vv. 17, 20, *in their context*, do not affirm that the righteous son will not suffer for the sins of his wicked father; they stress that in the great issues of

[1] See my *Men Spake from God*, p. 31, 36ff.

life, life and death, only the man's own actions are taken into consideration.

We should stress "all" in vv. 21, 24. Ezekiel is thinking neither of a periodic turning over of a new leaf with its short-lived reformation, which is fair enough while it lasts, nor of the temporary wavering of the righteous, who has found the temptations and trials of life too strong for him. He is thinking of a radical change to good or bad.

"Have I any pleasure in the death of the wicked?" The message of Ezekiel begins with the vision of the all-triumphant God visiting the exiles in their humiliation and shame; it shows the careful and loving marking out of the few righteous for preservation in the doomed city of Jerusalem; it gives the exiles the hope of transformation and glory (11: 17–20), and finally issues through destruction and judgment in the perfect establishment of God's will on earth. Nowhere in the Old Testament is the picture of sin blacker, of failure more complete than in Ezekiel, just because the prophet knows that the purpose of the God that condemns is salvation for all who will hear and turn.

A LAMENT (19: 1–14)

Though God had held out His promise of life to those exiles that would walk in His ways (ch. 18), there were two who could not benefit from it because of the sins of others, Jehoahaz and Jehoiachin, and so Ezekiel lifts up a lament over them.

There are numerous variations in the interpretation of this chapter, but this seems to be the only one that takes its position —due as I believe to Ezekiel himself—in the book seriously and does justice to it. This becomes the more obvious when we realize that the second half (vv. 10–14) comes in all probability from a slightly later date. Many see in these verses a prediction of the ruin of Zedekiah, but there is no claim that a prediction is being made. In addition it would involve the verbs in vv. 12–14 being taken as prophetic perfects,[1] but this idiom is seldom used unless the fact is made clear from the nature of the passage. It is far simpler to see two laments in the chapter; vv. 1–9 bewail the sad plight of Jehoahaz and Jehoiachin, while vv. 10–14, written after the fatal outcome of Zedekiah's rebellion, show its fatal effect on Jehoiachin's fortunes. In this way too the complete change of metaphor is most easily explained.

---

[1] To stress the certainty of the prediction, or the vividness of the vision the prophet often uses a "perfect" where a "future" would be expected. In most cases where a literal translation would create ambiguity the future has been used in English versions. The best known example of the prophetic perfect, translated as such, is Isa. 9: 6a, though in v. 6b our translations revert to futures, see also footnote to p. 80.

The mother (v. 2)—"What a lioness was your mother among lions!" (RSV)—is the kingdom of Judah. Jehoiakim is not mentioned because his fall was of his own creating. He was one of the most despicable of the descendants of David, for whom the only suitable fate was that he should "be buried with the burial of an ass" (Jer. 22: 19), i.e. no burial at all. Though it is not the reason for his omission, Ezekiel's imagery could in any case well dispense with him, for Jehoiakim had never been chosen king by his subjects (II King 23: 34).

As elsewhere in Ezekiel's allegories (cf. p. 61) we must avoid stressing the details. It is of no importance that Jehoahaz and Jehoiachin were, in fact, given little or no possibility of showing what they were capable of. Indeed, just here lies their tragedy. II Kings 23: 32; 24: 9 pass condemnation on them, but in the three months that each of them reigned there is no suggestion that either had merited his fate. Jeremiah strikes a similar note of regret in 22: 10ff. (Shallum = Jehoahaz) and 22: 24–30 (Coniah = Jeconiah = Jehoiachin). The young lion (*kepir*) is never a lion-cub but the lion in his first strength, cf. Isa. 31: 4; Amos 3: 4; Mic. 5: 8, etc.

Of Jehoahaz' fate we know nothing, and we may well assume that he did not long survive in Egypt Whether or not Zedekiah's rebellion made Jehoiachin's position worse we cannot be sure (cf. p. 19), but when he was finally released (II Kings 25: 27–30), it was as a broken man of fifty-five with no hope of restoration to his throne and with the right of succession for his decendants denied by God (Jer. 22: 29f., cf. I Chron. 3: 17). And so for the king in prison through the sin of his father and the criminal folly of his uncle Ezekiel laments in vv. 10–14.

The meaning has been obscured by textual difficulties. Already the rabbinic exegetes recognized that "in thy blood" (v. 10) is meaningless; "in a vineyard" (RSV) may be correct. A reference to RV mg. in v. 11 will show that the grammar in Hebrew is self-contradictory. RSV, which has the general support of LXX, will give the approximate force of what Ezekiel will have written:

> Its strongest stem became   a ruler's sceptre;
> it towered aloft   among the thick boughs;
> it was seen in its height   with the mass of its branches.

He is referring once again to Jehoiachin, under whom the vine was plucked up (v. 12). But the fire (v. 14) is Zekekiah—Ezekiel will not even call him a rod, or stem, just as he will not call him king (cf. p. 51).

CHAPTER IX

THE FAILURE OF ISRAEL

The Spiritual History of Israel (20: 1–44)

WITH ch. 20 we enter a new section of the book. In chs. 8–19 Ezekiel has been describing the sin of Jerusalem, but in chs. 20–23, which cover the period between the final drift into revolt (590 B.C.) and the appearing of the Babylonian armies before the walls of Jerusalem (24: 1—588 B.C.), while traversing much of the ground again, he goes deeper and seeks to lay bare the deeper reasons for Jerusalem's sin.

Ch. 20 is peculiarly important. Because the traditional interpretation of Israel's religion has with few exceptions consistently ignored it, it has failed to understand much in the prophetic books. This in turn opened the door to last century's destructive criticism, which was in other directions a travesty of the truth, even though it rescued much that traditionalism had lost. The general thought of the chapter was prepared for by ch. 16, but as Ezekiel is here unhampered by allegory, he is able to go far deeper and into more detail. For all that there is a certain curtain of verbal expression through which one has to win one's way before the meaning is clear. The chief difference between Ezekiel and traditional interpretation is briefly as follows. For tradition the idolatry and social unrighteousness of Israel that loom so large in the Old Testament were, until near the end, the exception; for Ezekiel a true knowledge of God and a true keeping of His law were so exceptional that he can ignore them.

Israel Cut Off from God (20: 1–4)

In certain aspects this section is reminiscent of 14: 1–11. There, however, God's refusal to answer the elders who enquire of Him is motivated by their sin; here God refuses to answer because they are the heirs of their ancestors (but see comments on vv. 30–32 below). The question (v. 4) has the force of an imperative, heightened by the repetition. The judging is carried out by rehearsing God's verdict on the past, cf. 22: 2 and especially 23: 36.

77

ISRAEL IN EGYPT (20: 5–9)

Ezekiel begins with the moment, when Moses returned to Egypt with the gracious message of Jehovah (Ex. 4: 29–31). In the light of Ezekiel it becomes easier to understand Moses' unwillingness to return and his expectation that his message would be refused (Ex. 4: 1). But Ezekiel's words need closer attention.

Though archæology has shown sporadic signs of Egyptian religious influence among the Israelites, it has shown clearly enough that it was never strong (cf. pp. 42 and 64). Nor does any passage of Scripture outside Ezekiel make any such suggestion. For Joshua the twin dangers were the gods of the Canaanites and the old traditional gods the Patriarchs had known beyond the Euphrates (Joshua 24: 14f.). Further, if we are to take the command in v. 7 literally, it seems strange that it is unmentioned in the story of the Exodus. The "idols of Egypt" are not the actual gods worshipped in Egypt, but the great uniformities of nature and human life they represented.

The plagues on Egypt are popularly interpreted as God's punishment, but such an explanation leaves many unsatisfied. They know that Pharaoh hardened his heart as well as having it hardened by God, but they cannot forget that God's threat of hardening was pronounced before Moses ever stood before Pharaoh (Ex. 4: 21; 7: 3). In addition the plagues seem excessive. But, though we cannot exclude the element of punishment, this was not the main intention of the plagues; they were demonstrations of Jehovah's power—see especially Ex. 9: 14ff., RV, and Paul's use of the passage in Rom. 9: 14–18—in particular over Egypt's gods (Ex. 12: 12). It should be reasonably obvious that this demonstration of Jehovah's power was for the good of the Israelites above all and in the first place.

Our conception of God has been so humanized and personalized by His revelation in Christ Jesus, that for the most part we fail to grasp the true nature of idolatry. The gods of the heathen were always forces of nature more or less thinly personified. In old Rome before the advent of Greek influence it is doubtful whether they had been personified at all. Even where we find figures like the Vedic Brihaspati, the "lord of prayer," the personified and deified sacrificial formula, or the Egyptian Thoth, the god of wisdom (and other things as well), they personify forces as real to the worshipper, even if less tangible, as the physical forces of nature.

There is probably no part of the world where nature presents a greater uniformity than in Egypt. Whether the rise of the

Nile was great or small, it occurred so regularly that it led the Egyptians to the making of what may have been the world's first regular calendar.[1] The sun and the river, life and death, these were the great facts to which man had to bow.

To us the three signs given to Moses (Ex. 4: 1–9) may seem too reminiscent of the conjurer's repertoire, and it is probably no accident that the Egyptian magicians were able to imitate two of them (Ex. 7: 11ff., 22). But to the Israelites, for whom they were intended, they were to proclaim that Jehovah controlled the uniformities of nature and was not controlled by them. This is even truer of the plagues. It has often been remarked that they were also blows at leading Egyptian gods (e.g. NBC, p. 112a), but this has hardly any meaning until we remember that the gods were the real power behind nature. Various unconvincing explanations have been given why Moses led the Israelites to the apparent trap facing the Sea of Reeds (English versions, "Red Sea"), but the obvious reason is that for Israel's sake it had to be crossed in a miraculous manner. In Semitic thought the sea was the type of chaos (the Babylonian Tiamat), the ancient enemy of the gods of cosmic order. The Israelites had to learn in this way that Jehovah was Lord of cosmos and chaos alike.

There is no evidence that the Israelites in Egypt ever questioned the existence of Jehovah or His call of the Patriarchs. It was rather that they doubted His power in the midst of the great uniformities of life. After the first flush of enthusiasm on Moses' return (Ex. 4: 31) their true feelings were revealed once the relentless pressure of daily life was felt again (Ex. 5: 21; 6: 9) or a new peril was faced (Ex. 14: 11f.). It is an interesting study, but outside the scope of this book, to see how this doubt of Jehovah's power dogged Israel throughout the Biblical period.

The typical orthodox Christian lays great stress on correct doctrine about God, but Israel's ancient sin is all too often his as well. It is not so difficult to trust, when all the old landmarks disappear and chaos seems to be resuming its sway, for then even the unbeliever is forced to throw himself on God, if he is to survive. It is amid the great uniformities of life, hemmed in by the great gods of "Egypt," the state, public opinion and economic pressure, that we find it hardest not to make concessions to the world.

Ezekiel stresses that the "natural" action of God would have been to punish Israel and finish with him then and there (v. 8). "I said" is far better rendered "I thought" (RSV), and so also

[1] Breasted: *Ancient Times*, p. 58f., suggests that the Egyptian calendar started in 4236 B.C., but this is far from enjoying universal acceptance.

in vv. 13, 21. The Bible never hesitates to use anthropo-
morphic language about God. His action (v. 9) based purely
on His character and for His glory represents His unchanging
purpose; His "thought" is what men would have considered
natural, right and proper, had He done it.

ISRAEL IN THE WILDERNESS (20: 10–26)

Ezekiel divides the wilderness period into two. In vv. 10–17
he is concerned with those who came out of Egypt and had
sentence of death passed on them at Kadesh Barnea (v. 15);
vv. 18–26 take up the fortunes of their children.

Of Israelite idolatry in the wilderness we know little. Joshua
24: 14f., is evidence enough that it must have been widespread
enough, even if secret, and Lev. 17: 7 shows one form it took—
the placating of the desert demons. Psa. 81: 12 and Acts 7: 42
point to its existence, as does indeed the warning of Deut. 4:
15–19—Acts 7: 43 has no bearing on this period, for it is a free
quotation of the LXX of Amos 5: 26, where a reference to the
RV mg. or RSV will show that it is referring to the prophet's
own time.[1]

Ezekiel's references to the Sabbath show that he was in possession of information that has not been preserved for us in the
Pentateuch. It need not surprise us, however. The drastic
and public punishment of the man who collected sticks on the
Sabbath (Num. 15: 32–36) suggests that a public example was
needed.

The modern tendency is to explain Ezekiel's stress on the
Sabbath by the peculiar needs of the exile, for Sabbath-keeping,
circumcision and the eating of "clean" food were among the
few outward elements of their religion that the exiles were able
to observe. This seems to be a mistake. No prophet rejected
the ritual and the external as whole-heartedly as did Jeremiah,
but we find the same stress on the Sabbath with him, and this
before the exile (Jer. 17: 19–27). We are so accustomed to a
weekly day of rest that probably only those that have lived in
pagan lands can grasp what life without it means, or what an
immense innovation it represented. In spite of strong arguments to the contrary, it seems conclusive from this chapter
and Neh. 9: 14 that the Sabbath is part of the Sinai revelation

---

[1] Some might challenge this opinion on the basis of Num. 23: 21. But
Balaam is not painting a picture of Israel as he is, but as God in His grace
regards him. In Deut. 32, the Song of Moses, all from v. 13 is prophetic, much
in the prophetic perfect, so vv. 16f. do not refer to wilderness idolatry; on the
other hand "There was no strange god with him" (v. 12b) means that Jehovah
had no other god to help Him.

and does not date from Eden. Certainly all efforts to find a trace of a weekly rest-day elsewhere in the ancient world have conspicuously failed. It is easy enough to keep the Sabbath in a legalistic way, but once it is correctly understood, it becomes a very real test of a man's faith. Only where the Lord is recognized as controller over the great powers of nature can one go beyond a legalistic cessation of work and turn heart and mind away from all the clamant claims of the world.

The reference in v. 23 is to Deut. 28: 15–68 (note especially v. 64). Just as the lack of faith and obedience in Egypt led inevitably to the disaster of the golden calf at Sinai and of Kadesh Barnea, so the failure of the second generation in the wilderness led inescapably to the exile of Israel and Judah. When Joshua said, " Ye cannot serve Jehovah" (Joshua 24: 19), he was basing himself on his knowledge of his hearers.

The Ebionite Christians of the first and second centuries A.D. used v. 25 in their polemic against the Jewish sacrificial system. They interpreted the verse to mean that much of the sacrificial law was a later, falsified addition.[1] We can hardly make the words bear this meaning, but equally they can hardly be interpreted literally. The vast bulk of the Mosaic legislation was given before the tragedy of Kadesh Barnea, and therefore could not be considered in any way a punishment of the younger wilderness generation and their descendants. In fact none of the legislation given after Kadesh Barnea can be said to have made any major modification in the Sinai legislation. We can only understand Ezekiel to mean that much of the law is so phrased and worded that only those with a true faith in and understanding of God would understand it aright. This seems, at least in part, to be the thought in Rom. 5: 20; Gal. 3: 19. Taken all in all we get the impression that the prophetic message was for most of its hearers sheer folly. They seem to have been as convinced that they were doing God's will by a formal keeping of the law as were the bulk of the Jews in our Lord's day. Ezekiel does not say that human sacrifice marked Israel's religion down through its history, but rather that it was the natural climax of its downward path (see p. 63), and therefore an indication of the essential wrongness of all that had gone before. But the very degradation brought about by their lack of understanding was to drive them back to God (v. 26). As Paul says, "The law was like a strict governess in charge of us until we went to the school of Christ and learned to be justified by faith in Him" (Gal. 3: 24).[2]

[1] Schoeps: *Theologie und Geschichte des Judenchristentums*, pp. 151, 221.

[2] Phillips: *Letters to Young Churches*.

F

It may well be asked how this gloomy judgment can be reconciled with the idyllic picture of Hos. 2: 15; 9: 10a; Jer. 2: 2f.; Ezek. 16: 8–14. Compared to what Israel was to become, the prophets could well look back to the wilderness period, in spite of all its faults, as the happiest time in Israel's history. But when the prophet had to trace the poison root that led to the bitter fruit, he had to show it there right at the beginning. Incidentally, how often do we think of the Wilderness Wanderings as the happiest time in Israel's history?

Israel in the Land (20: 27–29)

This section of the prophecy is kept short because all the false religion of the time of the Judges and under the monarchy was merely the natural outcome of what had gone before. Ezekiel had already described it in 16: 15–34 (cf. p. 63). Now Ezekiel dismisses the whole of this man-made perversion by a pun (v. 29a) based apparently on popular etymology (v. 29b). He links *Bamah*—consistently and conveniently, but not quite adequately rendered "high place"[1]—with *"mah* (what) is *ha-Bamah* (the high place) whereunto *ha-ba'im* (ye go)?" In other words he suggests that the very popular etymology showed that men recognized that the *bamah* and all it symbolized was merely a place of human choice and not of Divine ordaining.

Ezekiel's Own Generation (20: 30–32)

Seeing we lack confirmatory evidence, we should not infer from v. 31 that human sacrifices were brought in again after the death of Josiah. Note that it is not included among the abominations of Jerusalem in ch. 8. We may rather compare it with a saying like that of Matt. 23: 29–35; Luke 11: 47–51. Josiah's reformation had not meant any real break with the past, and given the opportunity the sins of the past would lift their heads again. The real temptation for Ezekiel's contemporaries was dully to acquiesce in that which had happened and to adopt the idolatry of the places of their exile (v. 32). Their very misunderstanding of the nature and will of Jehovah would make such a step easy.

Jehovah's Triumph (20: 33–44)

The whole of the chapter up till now has been seeking to establish one point: once God chose Israel for His own purposes,

[1] See note on I Kings 3: 2 in ICC or NBC, or more fully in Albright: *Archaeology and the Religion of Israel*, p. 105ff.

nothing that Israel could do could thwart Him in working out His final will, however much He might have to discard generation after generation on the way. Now Ezekiel proclaims that the last act of the strange drama was to be played out.

Jeremiah had already said that Israel's history had been worked out under a broken covenant: "Behold, the days come, saith Jehovah, that I will make a new covenant with the house of Israel and with the house of Judah: not according to the covenant I made with their fathers in the day that I took them by the hand to bring them out of the land of Egypt; forasmuch as they broke My covenant and I had to lord it over them (*ba'alti bam*)" Jer. 31: 31f., so essentially RV mg. Now He would be king over them in judgment (v. 33f.). As once before, there would be a testing in the wilderness—of the exile (v. 35) —and a judgment that would separate His true people from the idolaters. We can best render v. 39: "Go, serve each his idols, and afterwards, if ye do not obey Me—!" (ICC). Many of the exiles must have adopted the idolatry around them, but they vanished without trace. It is not easy to decide whether we should follow the Hebrew in v. 37, "the bond of the covenant," or the LXX, "by number" (RSV).

As we have previously noticed (p. 73), Ezekiel's vision of the future is foreshortened, and centuries and a yet greater exile in "the wilderness of the peoples" would have to elapse before God's purpose with Israel would be fulfilled. For all that vv. 40–44 have had a striking partial fulfilment. The remnant that returned under Sheshbazzar, Zerubbabel, and Joshua had learnt certain aspects of Ezekiel's teaching well, and it was reinforced about a century later by the work of Ezra. Even though it was often not according to knowledge, there was a real zeal for God. The Judaism of the return provided the setting in which the Christ could come and the Church be born, while the amazingly rapid spread of Christianity in the first century of its existence was in large measure due to the manner in which the Synagogue had prepared the way for it among the Gentiles. This partial fulfilment gives us confidence to look forward to the day when "all Israel shall be saved" (cf. p. 129).

CHAPTER X

THE BLOODY CITY

THE SWORD OF THE LORD (20:45 – 21:32)

THE chapter division is unfortunate, for this is one section,
as is duly recognized in the Hebrew. It consists of four
oracles all, except perhaps the last, spoken during the
time that Nebuchadnezzar was on his way to subdue the revolts
that had broken out in Tyre, Ammon and Jerusalem. The
language is at times far from easy, and our understanding is
made the more difficult by a number of textual corruptions.

THE SWORD OF THE LORD IS DRAWN (20:45 – 21:7)

This oracle falls into two. In 20: 45–49 we have a very
figurative description of the coming destruction of Jerusalem
under the picture of a forest fire. In 21: 1–7 it is explained;
though still in figurative language, its meaning is obvious.

In v. 46 three words are used for "south." Two are merely
variants used for effect, but the third, differentiated in the RV
by the use of a capital letter, is best translated, as in the RSV,
by Negeb, the dry semi-wilderness of the south of Judea.
Ezekiel is told to "set his face toward the south," for though
Judea lay to the west of Tel-abib, Ezekiel has been transported
in spirit to the Chaldean army, which is now marching south
from Carchemish and the Euphrates. The Negeb being a semi-
arid area, a fire in its dry shrubs (the forest is little more than
that) is a very serious matter and extremely difficult to put
out.

As I pointed out in connexion with 2: 8–3: 3 (p. 28), the
divine word has to be assimilated by the prophet before it is
spoken, and therefore it shows the peculiarities of the individual
prophet. On the other hand the prophet has no liberty to
recast the message into a form more acceptable to him and his
hearers. This is shown by v. 49. While Ezekiel's fellow-exiles
might well not understand the details of such an oracle, the
general intention must have been obvious. But they showed a
trait we are all familiar with today. As now so then, because
something in the Word was obscure, it was taken as an excuse
for ignoring the whole message.

The use of the forest fire as an image is explained in v. 3. Once the sword of the Lord was drawn it would slay as indiscriminately as a forest fire destroys. No contradiction should be seen between this verse and 9: 4–6 or ch. 18, though this latter is addressed principally to the exiles. Emerson was near the truth, when he wrote, "A foolish consistency is the hobgoblin of little minds, adored by little statesmen and philosophers and divines." The Scriptures are never self-contradictory, but they often seem to be inconsistent, and the worst examples of foolishness in exegesis are due to those who could not or would not grasp this. Only God and His angels know who bears the secret mark, only God can pass the judgment as to who is really walking in His ways. For man with his biased judgments there will be good who will perish and evil who will be spared. But Ezekiel does not have to explain this. If any will misunderstand, let him misunderstand!

Ezekiel was evidently given a vision of the destruction and this broke him down (v. 6f.). The prophet was seldom if ever a passive recipient of his visions, cf. Amos 7: 2, 5; Jer. 4: 19ff.; 31: 26.

The Song of the Sword (21: 8–17)

The language is often difficult. RSV seems to make the only possible sense of v. 10b, "Or do we make mirth?"—i.e. is the warning a mere joke?—"You have despised the rod, my son, with everything of wood"—i.e. all lesser chastisement has been despised. But it would be dangerous to assume that the text is in order. The same is even more true of the RSV in vv. 14–16; it at least makes sense, which can hardly be said of AV and RV: "Prophesy therefore, son of man; clap your hands and let the sword come down twice, yea thrice, the sword for those to be slain; it is the sword for the great slaughter, which encompasses them, that their hearts may melt, and many fall at their gates. I have given the glittering sword; ah! it is made like lightning, it is polished for slaughter. Cut sharply to right and left where your edge is directed." The exultation of the prophet in this oracle contrasts strangely with his distress in v. 6f., but this must always be the effect of God's judgments on the believer. His heart exults because God is triumphing, but it breaks because of those who perish under His judgments.

Nebuchadnezzar is the Sword of the Lord (21: 18–27)

RSV gets the sense in v. 19 by rendering "mark two ways"; the prophecy was obviously accompanied by a symbolic action.

someone. The RSV "... all the house of Israel who are in it"
is probably correct.

In our study of ch. 34 we shall see why the Messianic king is
called "prince" (*nasi'*) in the prophecy of the restoration, but
Ezekiel's reason for using *nasi'* of Zedekiah is another. He
never calls him king (*melek*) as he does Jehoiachin (17: 12), cf.
21: 25, for the general description in 7: 27 can hardly be
regarded as an exception to this statement.

The clue is given by the only other use of *nasi'* for a reigning
king, viz. I Kings 11: 34, where it is applied to Solomon.
Clearly the implication there is that Solomon had forfeited his
right to be king by reason of his sin. Ezekiel regarded Jehoiachin as the true king (cf. p. 16 and 17:13): the Judæan kingship had ended with his exile and therefore the exiles could not
put any hope on him. This is the attitude of the Chronicler as
well, as may be deduced from the way he dismisses Zedekiah's
reign (II Chron. 36:11ff.). Ezekiel may well have been influenced too by his foreknowledge of Zedekiah's broken oath (see
notes on ch. 17).

The acted fate of Zedekiah was followed by the acting out of
the fate of the people (vv. 17–20); this section is largely a repetition of 4: 9–12. But while there the stress was on the small
quantities carefully measured, here it is on the dismay and
anxiety with which his rations were eaten. We are not told
how Ezekiel expressed these emotions, but he was doubtless
able to communicate them vividly.

THE PROBLEM OF PROPHETS AND OF PROPHECY
(12:21 – 14:11)

There is nothing easier than being wise after the event, but
we generally take to ourselves unmerited credit for being it.
It is in that spirit that we are apt to be unsparing in our condemnation of the Israelites of old for their rejection of the
prophetic message. We normally forget that for the average
man things were not quite so simple as we imagine. We picture
men like Jeremiah and Ezekiel as isolated, lonely, unique, but
to their contemporaries they were merely eccentric members of
the fairly large company of the prophets. That which distinguished them in public thought from the other prophets was
mainly that they had a message of unrelieved doom, whereas
the others preached hope and peace.

It is most important that we should realize this. The phrase
"false prophets" is one of the New Testament, not of the Old.
They are never presented to us as just deliberate frauds, and

As far south as Riblah Nebuchadnezzar would use the same road whether he was marching against Ammon or Jerusalem. Ezekiel depicts the scene at the road-fork where the Babylonian king has to make up his mind which of the rebels is to feel the weight of his chastisement first. AV has partly missed the force of v. 21. Nebuchadnezzar uses three means of divination: arrows with names written on them are thrown in a certain way and "into his hand comes the lot (i.e. arrow) for Jerusalem" (v. 22 RSV); he consults the age-old magic means of the *teraphim* (almost certainly to be understood as one object in spite of the plural form, possibly as in rabbinic tradition a mummied child's head); he sacrifices and looks at the liver, perhaps the commonest of Babylonian forms of divination.

v. 23 is difficult. The people of Jerusalem do not take the result of the divination seriously, but why? It is not clear who has sworn oaths to whom. It may be that the old interpretation represented by some MSS. of LXX, by the Targum, Aquila, Theodotion and the Vulgate is correct, "they have weeks upon weeks," i.e. the Chaldean is in no hurry.

The confidence is baseless, for the time of reckoning of the "unhallowed wicked one, prince of Israel" (v. 25, RSV) has come. For "prince," not king, see p. 51). The mitre (v. 26—the AV "diadem" is impossible) is otherwise in the Old Testament a priestly garment only (Ex. 28: 4). Though we are not otherwise told so—but we are really told very little about the actions of Zedekiah—it may well be that this weak man had given way to the temptation that always dogged the kings of Judah and Israel and had claimed to be the head of the church as well as of the state, a position held both by the Pharaoh and the king of Babylon.[1]

With the fall of Zedekiah the old order was to pass never to be restored until the Messiah came. Such is the obvious meaning of v. 27. In the slightly enigmatic "until he come whose right it is' we have almost certainly the first extant interpretation of Shiloh in Gen. 49: 10 that has come down to us. The interpretation of Shiloh as a proper name was a rarity before 1534. Ezekiel reads the word *shelloh*=whose it is. It is gratifying that RSV should have rendered "until he comes to whom it belongs" in Gen. 49: 10 instead of the transliteration, which is really meaningless. Ezekiel's interpretation is supported "by nearly all Versions."[2]

[1] Reference may be made to NBC, p. 335b, also to 312b.

[2] Skinner: *Genesis* (ICC), p. 523.

The Sword of Ammon (21: 28–32)

The Ammonites, freed from immediate alarm by Nebuchadnezzar's march against Jerusalem instead of Rabbah, seem to
have sought to appease him by attacking Judah.   But their
sword had not been chosen by the Lord to do His work, and so
their attack will only bring judgment on them.   Note God's
command in v. 30; the question of AV is incorrect.   The theme
is taken up again in ch. 25.

The Bloody City (22: 1–16)

The word "blood" occurs no less than seven times in these
sixteen verses.   One gets the impression that in the vision
accompanying the words Ezekiel saw the city he knew so well
through a shimmer of blood.

Because of that concreteness in Hebrew outlook which made
it natural for one factor to be considered at a time, as though it
were the whole of the truth, many Western expositors have
been misled into thinking that verses like Lev. 17: 11; Gen. 9: 4,
etc., teach that the life principle is peculiarly in the blood.   But
as a fundamental passage like Gen. 2: 7 clearly implies, the Old
Testament equally recognizes the role of breath, or spirit, in
giving and preserving life.

But while a man's breath symbolized above all man's life
being lived, e.g. Isa. 2: 22; Job 27: 3; 33: 4, for it is from a man's
breathing that we best know him to be alive, and the more
vigorous that life the deeper the breathing, his blood symbolized
above all his life taken by violence.[1]   God is the giver of life,
which is outside man's power to bestow.   For that reason the
taking of life, symbolically expressed by "the shedding of
blood," except by God's permission or command, was supremely
an insult to Him.

This explains the to us rather enigmatic legislation of Deut.
19: 1–13.   It has no typical meaning that I have been able to
discover, and it can only imperfectly be explained as a means
for curbing the traditional blood feud.   By freeing the uninten-
tional manslayer from civil punishment, but by submitting him
to extreme civil inconvenience, possibly for the rest of his life,
it is intended to stress what the taking of life means to *God*.
The modern indifference to deaths on the road is doubtless a
major pointer to the extent to which we have lost the Biblical
outlook on life.   This reverence for life as God's gift is in part

[1] There is an excellent treatment of this subject in Stibbs: *The Meaning of
the Word "Blood" in Scripture* (Tyndale Press).

the motivation for the legislation of Lev. 17: 1–7, for its abrogation in Deut. 12: 20–25 is only permissive; the ideal was still that an animal killed for food should be brought as a peace offering.

It is from this standpoint that we have to understand the list of sins with which Jerusalem is charged in this section. It is called "the bloody city" (v. 2), not because murder was so frequent, or because it was the worst of its sins, but because all the sins with which it is charged are sins against the true life of man and so infallibly destroy the society in which they are tolerated. This explains the linking with it of the general charge of idolatry (v. 3). The form of idolatry to which Israel was most prone was the reducing of Jehovah to the level of a nature god (see pp. 36 and 63). Death is as much a feature of nature as birth, so nature religions have no place for reverence for life as such. The apparent exceptions of higher Hinduism and of Buddhism are due to other reasons; in them it is no question of reverence for life as God's gift.

The first group of sins includes judicial murder (v. 6), doubtless for allegedly high purposes of state, and the perversion of justice by bribery and false witness (vv. 7, 9, 12). The princes (*nasi'*) may refer to the heads of the great families, but in the light of the use of the word in 12: 12 (see p. 51) it more likely refers to the corrupter kings.

It would be dangerous anywhere in the Old Testament to demand a purely literal interpretation of vv. 9a and 12a, and this is particularly the case in Ezekiel. If we may at all judge from passages like Amos 2: 6f.; Isa. 5: 8; Mic. 2: 2 (and cf. I Kings 21), the driving motive behind most judicial unrighteousness in Israel was the desire to obtain land. But the landless man was virtually an outcast, with little other possibility of keeping alive than by selling himself into slavery, from which there would be no release, for Jer. 34: 8–22 shows that the law of Ex. 21:2, Deut. 15: 12 was seldom observed at this period. But even if he did manage to eke out a living as a free man, the very vehemence of Naboth in his refusal to sell his vineyard (I Kings 21: 3) shows that separated from his patrimony a man lost an essential part of his dignity and standing.

The same principle holds good for v. 7b, c. Apart from the constant stress in the prophets on God's demand for justice for the stranger, orphan and widow, we have the explicit commands in Deut. 24: 17; 27: 19, and above all and most strikingly Ex. 22: 21–24. The stranger (*ger*, not *nokri* or *zar*) is not a foreigner passing through the country, but one permitted to live in it, i.e. one separated from his natural protectors and

dependent on the justice of those in whose midst he lives.   For
that reason the verb *gur* can be used of the Levite (Deut. 18: 6;
Judges 17: 7; 19: 1) and even of an Israelite living outside his
own tribe (Judges 19: 16).   The orphan and the widow refer
not primarily to those that have lost their natural protectors,
but to those who in addition have none to take their place.   So
the maladministration of justice is seen through the shimmer of
blood, for those that suffered from it were driven to the bitter
straits so graphically described in Job 24: 4–12; 30: 2–7.

The same holds good of usury (v. 12).   In an agricultural
community subject to frequent droughts, locust swarms, etc.,
many were chronically undernourished, and very few had adequate reserves.   So any major loan, even if there was no interest
to pay, was an almost unsupportable burden, hence the legislation of Deut. 15: 1f.   To add interest however small—and it
was frequently large—was both to break the Divine law and
the debtor.

In the deepest spiritual sense the other sins enumerated also
lead to "bloodshed," for they lead to an inevitable collapse of
society.   Little more than their enumeration is needed.
There is in v. 7 the treating of parents with contempt (RSV),
treated as a capital offence bringing God's curse with it in Ex.
21: 17; Lev. 20: 9; Deut. 27: 16.   With this is quite naturally
linked a contempt of God's requirements (v. 8).   Finally we
have a group of sexual sins (vv. 9b–11) which cannot find any
cloak or excuse in the strength of fallen man's passions, and
which destroy the very pillars of society.   The eating upon the
mountains (v. 9) refers to the orgiastic feasts in the semi-
Canaanized high places in which sexual promiscuity played a
large part.   Sexual promiscuity is always a tremendous evil.
Blake was hardly exaggerating when he wrote,

> The Harlot's cry from Street to Street
> Shall weave Old England's winding Sheet.

But when as among the Canaanites—this was "the iniquity of
the Amorite" (Gen. 15: 16)—it receives the blessing of religion,
there is no deadlier danger to the individual and society.
Nothing need be added about the various forms of incest.   What
needs to be stressed is that Ezekiel sees in offences against the
natural modesties of sex (v. 10b) and in adultery (v. 11a) evils
as great and as deadly as incest and promiscuity of the worst
sort.   We need not then be surprised that today, when adultery
finds many an apologist, unnatural vice is steadily increasing.

For v. 2a see the note on 20: 4: "I have smitten mine hand"
(v. 13)—"I strike my hands together" (RSV)—a gesture of

scorn, cf. 6: 11; 21: 14, 17. "I will consume thy filthiness out of thee" (v. 15): the following section, though perhaps originally a separate prophecy, explains the implications of this somewhat enigmatic threat. "Thou shalt be profaned in thyself" (v. 16, RV, AV mg.—the AV text is impossible) is hard to explain; RSV is probably correct in following LXX, Syriac and Vulgate in rendering "I shall be profaned through you" (so ICC, Cam. B., NBC). The profanation was not so much through the evil life of the survivors of the sack of Jerusalem as through the nations believing that Jehovah had not been able to protect His own people and temple.

JERUSALEM THE SMELTER'S FURNACE (22: 17–22)

This oracle is reminiscent of Jer. 6: 27–30. Ezekiel is not concerned, as is Zech. 13: 9; Mal. 3: 2f. with God's purifying and refining of His people, but with demonstrating that there is nothing there to be refined. This gives the true meaning to the threat in v. 15. Such a purification meant the blotting out of the survivors, for there was only filthiness in them. In the meantime this was to be demonstrated in Jerusalem's last agony.

THE CORRUPTION OF THE PEOPLE (22: 23–31)

This oracle is addressed to Jerusalem, the "her" of v. 24. ICC argues that the phrase "in the day of indignation" (v. 24) refers to the destruction of Jerusalem, and so this is an oracle looking back and explaining God's action. Though I have no objection in principle to such a view, as may be seen from my treatment of 16: 53–63 (p. 67), I consider it unnecessary here. "The day of indignation" for Judah began when Josiah fell in 609 at Megiddo. This is one of the main thoughts of Jeremiah, and Ezekiel is trying to hammer it home all the time. The yet future destruction of the city was something inevitable, the mere conclusion of a process begun a generation earlier. The past tenses of this section are not referring to the last anguished years of Jerusalem in particular, but to the whole century and a half of decline from Ahaz on, a decline only temporarily held up by the outward reforms of Hezekiah and Josiah. Though it is hardly necessary, the tenses of v. 31 can be explained as prophetic perfects (see footnote, p. 75).

Though we might compare v. 25 with Mic. 3: 5, there is no real similarity, and the verse stands without any true parallel. There seems little doubt that we should read "princes" (*nesi'im* for *nebi'im*) with LXX, RSV, ICC, Cam. B., NBC and interpret the word as in v. 6. The princes (*sarim*) of v. 27 are the great men of the land; the translation prince—208 times, captain 125 times, 12 other renderings 84 times—is in so far misleading that no blood connexion with the royal house is implied, though those we call princes might well be numbered among the *sarim*.

We must not imagine that, when Ezekiel condemns the priests (v. 26), he is suggesting that their ritual neglects are in the same category of iniquity as the outrages on justice by the kings and their great men. His willingness to place the moral and the ritual side by side in this way has been the cause of the most frequent misunderstanding of his message. It is not the people but the priests he is condemning. He has no interest in seeing unrighteous princes keeping the ritual laws of purity. But the priests by their indifference to and neglect of that portion of the Divine law which only they could expound, showed their lack of respect for God and thereby lost their ability to restrain the unrighteousness of the mighty. The prophets have been sufficiently dealt with in the notes on 13: 7, 10 (p. 55).

The people of the land (v. 29) are here almost certainly "the free, property-owning, full citizens of Judah."[1] The phrase, *'am ha-'aretz*, changed its meaning down the centuries, but it was probably always used in a technical sense, and here it will have the same meaning as in II Kings 11: 14, 18; 21: 24; 23: 30, 35; 25: 19. These free farmers were zealots for the old order as against the court circles in Jerusalem, but their zeal did not extend to doing the will of God. Fanaticism and righteousness seldom find themselves bedfellows.

ICC interprets v. 30 of the lack of a prophet. While the language suits the interpretation, the historical situation does not. If ever a single prophetic figure could have turned away the wrath of God, it would have been Jeremiah, but he was not even able to postpone the judgment on Jerusalem. It is far more likely that Ezekiel is thinking of the kings. The downward course of Judah began in earnest after the death of Jehoshaphat. In the long story of decline the names of Hezekiah and Josiah stand out as apparent factors for good. But when we see them through the eyes of Isaiah and Jeremiah, we find that however saintly and earnest they may have been in their private lives, they were quite incapable of leading their reformations from the external to the internal, and indeed there is no indication that they saw any necessity for it. Ezekiel seems to suggest that this failure was one of character, and with it Jerusalem was doomed (cf. also pp. 119ff).

[1] von Rad: *Studies in Deuteronomy*, p. 63: see also NBC ,p. 323b.

OHOLAH AND OHOLIBAH (CH. 23)

It is often assumed that this chapter is merely a variant of the theme of ch. 16, in which the grossness of detail is heightened to bring out the enormity of Israel's sin.   In fact the main thought in the two chapters is quite dissimilar.   In the former it was the corruption of Israel's religion and its descent into idolatry that was under consideration.   Here it is the unfaithfulness of Israel as revealed in its relation to other nations that is being condemned.

Contrary to the view that used to be so popular a short time ago, it is now realized that the gods of the heathen neighbours of Israel were considered by them to be rulers of the whole world.   Though their sway, so far as their functions in nature were concerned, was universal, they had divided out their earthly domain among themselves, thus explaining why a certain god or goddess was in a special way the god of a city or country.   Though the gods acted together to prevent the re-entrance of chaos, and one of their number was recognized as their king, yet they had their family quarrels and fights in which even the kingship could pass from one god to another. Wars on the earth were the earthly reflection of these struggles in heaven, and the making of peace and alliances inevitably involved gods as well as men.

This is why all alliances made by Israel were anathema to the prophets, especially when they were made with great powers. The humble status of the ambassadors of Israel as they stood before the great kings of Egypt or Assyria, or Nebuchadnezzar was in the eyes of the world only the earthly counterpart of Jehovah's lowly status as He begged Amon, or Ashur, or Marduk for help.   It is not to be understood that the prophets thought that anything of the sort happened; the gods of the nations had no real existence for them.   But they judged the actions of their contemporaries, as so often in the Bible, by what they meant to those that did them.   In Israel, as in the Church, to turn to any outside power for help meant that there were other powers beside Jehovah, and that He was not able to win the victory by Himself.   Hence all such alliances are unfaithfulness of the worst type, or in the language of the allegory sheer harlotry.

Unlike the allegory in ch. 16 both kingdoms are introduced in detail, because, while the religious declension took somewhat different forms in the two kingdoms, and hence it might be argued that Israel was not really a warning to Judah—but see Jer. 3: 6–13, where the picture of the two wives of Jehovah is

used to underline the guilt of Judah's corrupted religion—as
there was no difference in their foreign policy, there was no
excuse for Judah's not learning from the fate of Israel.

The mention of Egypt must surely be understood in much
the same way as it was interpreted in 20: 7f., cf. also 16: 26 (pp.
78 and 64). The earliest political alliance of any kind we know
of between Israel and Egypt was that created by Solomon's
marriage to Pharaoh's daughter (I Kings 3: 1), but that cannot
possibly be meant here. Just as in ch. 20 Ezekiel implies that
amid the great uniformities of nature in Egypt Israel came to
doubt Jehovah's power to control nature (cf. p. 79), so in the
highly organized state of Egypt Israel was so impressed by its
organized power, that it doubted Jehovah's ability to triumph
without human order and power to succour Him. This lies
behind the cry, "Make us a king to judge us *like all the nations*"
(I Sam. 8: 5), and Solomon's bolstering up of his kingdom by
marriage alliances with neighbouring states.

Oholah's *voluntary* association with the Assyrians (v. 5) refers
probably to Jehu's payment of tribute to Shalmaneser III in
841 B.C.[1] This was almost certainly an act of discretion rather
than of necessity. Then Israel's temporary rise in power under
Jehoash (II Kings 13: 25) and Jeroboam II (II Kings 14: 25,
28) was quite possibly helped by alliance with Assyria. Oholibah's association with Assyria (v. 12) refers of course to Ahaz'
placing of Judah under the protection of Tiglath-pileser III
(II Kings 16: 7–10) in spite of the pleading of Isaiah (Isa.
7: 3–17). Her association with the Chaldeans (vv. 14–16) does
not refer to events in the lifetime of Ezekiel, but to the episode
of Merodach-baladan in the days of Hezekiah (II Kings
20: 12–19; Isa. 39). True enough we are left to infer that the
first overtures came from Merodach-baladan, but they would
hardly have been risked, if there had not been good grounds
for thinking that they would be welcome. We must never
minimize the doom pronounced by Isaiah (II Kings 20: 17f.;
Isa. 39: 6f.); Hezekiah's act was a far more serious one than the
superficial reader might imagine.[2]

---

[1] An event not recorded in the Bible. Evidence for it is found on the black
obelisk of Shalmaneser III now in the British Museum. For details see any
work on Biblical archaeology.

[2] The Chaldeans were a tribe living in the marshy country at the head of the
Persian Gulf. Owing to the difficulty of the terrain the Assyrians probably
never completely subdued them. On a number of occasions they were able to
gain control of Babylon and resist Assyria from there. Nabopolassar, the
father of Nebuchadnezzar, who finally freed Babylon and then in alliance with
the Medes destroyed Nineveh, was a Chaldean. Hence the Chaldeans are
sometimes equated with Babylon, sometimes distinguished from it.

Four threats are uttered against Oholibah:

(i) In vv. 22–27 her Chaldean "lovers" come to judge her, with their conquered vassals in their train, Pekod, Shoa, Koa and Assyria.

(ii) We find in vv. 28–31 an explanation why her "lovers" should thus deal with her. They have become those "whom thou hatest." Oholibah had not even the excuse of adulterous passion in her disloyalty to Jehovah. Her overtures to the Chaldeans had been merely the calculated self-interest of the harlot. And so we pass over to another thought: calculated disloyalty leads to idolatry (v. 30).

(iii) The cup of God's wrath (vv. 32–34); this idea is to be found in Jer. 25: 15–31; 49: 12; Lam. 4: 21; Hab. 2: 16; Obad. 16; Isa. 51: 17, 22f.; Psa. 75: 8. Though the concept may not be quite the same in all these cases, it is clear that the effect of drinking the wine of God's wrath is above all to cause madness and ruin. It seems to symbolize above all God's forcing man to partake of the full harvest of his deeds; the wine of God's wrath is pressed from the vines of man's own planting and cultivation.

(iv) The final threat in v. 35 is by its very brevity the worst. Oholibah is to be left to herself. Greater punishment for the sinner does not exist.

The concluding portion of the chapter vv. 36–49 is an independent prophecy which serves as a sort of appendix. It is not easy to interpret, and ICC may be correct in suggesting that it may have been called forth by some particular incident in the last desperate straits of the city. In our ignorance of these circumstances the oracle ceases to be luminous. It clearly stresses, however, that the outcome of political entanglements and faithlessness to Jehovah is idolatry and the worst forms of pagan worship. Why both the sisters should appear here does not seem to be clear.

Some have found difficulty in two sisters being depicted as Jehovah's wives, for this was prohibited in the law (Lev. 18: 18). But we have the same picture in Jer. 3: 6ff. The simple answer seems to be that when the Israelites used metaphor and simile of God and His relations to His people, they were never carried away by them and always remembered that they were no more than convenient approximations to the truth. That Israel was Jehovah's bride was a common prophetic picture from Hosea onward. Since both Israel and Judah were His, it was looked on as natural to speak of both of them as God's wife. But behind the picture of the dual marriage was the firm knowledge that it was only as part of "all Israel" that either kingdom could claim any such relationship to Jehovah. In other words this allegory chooses a picture to serve a purpose, but it makes no claim that this picture is in all respects a theologically true one. We may never in Old or New Testament stress the *subsidiary* points of allegory or parable.

CHAPTER XI

THE MIDNIGHT HOUR

THE BLOW FALLS (24: 1–27)

IN January 588 B.C., when Jehoiachin's captivity had lasted almost ten years (v. 1), Zedekiah's plots and treacheries had their reward, and Nebuchadnezzar's army ringed Jerusalem for its last agony. The iron ring was to relax for a few weeks to deal with the relieving army of Pharaoh Apries (Jer. 34: 21f.; 37: 5, 11), but it is doubtful whether it even waited for a battle. Certainly the Egyptians were soon back over their frontier (Jer. 37: 7), and they did not stir again to save their Judean allies from their fate.

On the very day that Jerusalem was invested—cf. v. 1 with II Kings 25: 1; Jer. 39: 1—God revealed the fact to Ezekiel and ordered him to make a special note of the date. It is not likely that this was to enhance Ezekiel's reputation as a prophet. It was rather to anticipate and prevent any later suggestion that the siege and capture of Jerusalem could have been due to some passing inattention and carelessness on Jehovah's part (cf. I Kings 18: 27).

It is impossible to be sure whether the remainder of the chapter is to be looked on as happening on the day on which the siege began and on the next, or whether it extends over some time. We have earlier seen that the dates prefixed to the sections of the prophecy need only apply to the first oracle in the section; the remainder may extend up to the next recorded date. In view, however, of the general impression given, it is probably best to assume that the whole chapter is to be dated on the tenth and eleventh days of the tenth month.

THE PARABLE OF THE POT (24: 3–14)

Though it is not necessary, it is probable that we should picture Ezekiel acting out his words, for the pot of the parable is a common cooking pot, in which a whole lamb could easily be cooked. "Take the choicest one of the flock" (v. 5, RSV) is the correct rendering; it should be obvious that we should continue, "Pile the logs under it" (RSV). This is demanded by common sense and v. 10; the error is due to dittography in the Hebrew, i.e. a letter has been written twice instead of only once.

The message in vv. 3–5 is a complete one, for it graphically depicts the extreme straits of the besieged. In v. 6 we pass over to Jerusalem itself, symbolized by the cooking pot. The fate of the besieged is glanced at in v. 6b; RSV seems to get the meaning, when it renders the final words "without making any choice." If we assume that Ezekiel has been acting out his message, then the rust-marks on the cooking pot (the AV "scum" should be ignored) remind him of blood-stains, and we are back in thought in ch. 22: 1–16. By v. 7 Ezekiel is stressing Jerusalem's completely callous and casual attitude towards murder, however brought about. Lev. 17: 13 is sufficient comment on v. 7c. In fact it was a very widespread belief that blood that had not been covered cried aloud for vengeance, cf. Job 16: 18, and in part Gen. 4: 10; Isa. 26: 21.

God now (v. 9) returns to the original thought of the prophecy, but pictures Himself as making up the fire. As a result the contents, apparently, are not merely well cooked and unceremoniously dealt with, but actually destroyed. The best translation of the difficult Hebrew of v. 10 would seem to be, "Multiply the logs, kindle the fire, make an end of the flesh, and empty out the broth, and let the bones be burned up." Once the contents are destroyed the empty pot is replaced on the flames until it melts as the only way of getting rid of the rust (v. 11). It is difficult to interpret v. 12; RV mg. and RSV are superior to RV tx. and AV, but they are probably only approximations to the meaning.

THE DEATH OF EZEKIEL'S WIFE (24: 15–24)

If the suggestion made above is correct, the revelation of his wife's coming death will have come to Ezekiel, while the people were still gathered round him listening to the parable of the pot. God prohibited all the normal outward forms of mourning to Ezekiel (vv. 16f.). "The bread of men" means ordinary bread, i.e. the bread that mourners were accustomed to eat. So the RSV "the bread of mourners" is justified.

It is easy enough to motivate God's prohibition, so far as Ezekiel is concerned. The loss of his wife was but a trifle compared to the coming destruction of the sanctuary (v. 21), and if we wished, we could find a loose parallel in Jer. 16: 1–9. But this does not explain why the exiles will not mourn, when the news of the destruction of Jerusalem is received. The explanation in NBC that this is a Divine prohibition of mourning is

G

quite impossible. The suggestion of ICC and Cam. B. that the shock will be too stunning for tears will hardly bear investigation, and in the light of Ezekiel's continued warnings and of the occasional rumour that must have filtered through, it is questionable whether the shock will really have been so great. There is, however, an explanation which is reasonable in itself and which really establishes the parallel between Ezekiel and the exiles.

Zedekiah's revolt must have meant a very considerable aggravation in the position of the Judean exiles. They will all automatically have come under suspicion as potential rebels, cf. the drastic treatment some years earlier of Ahab and Zedekiah (Jer. 29: 21f.) for prophecy which was probably only by inference treasonable (cf. p. 31). Any outward manifestation of grief over the chastisement of rebels against whom Nebuchadnezzar felt especially strongly could only have received the worst interpretation. In other words there will have been the implicit official prohibition of mourning which is parallel to God's explicit prohibition to Ezekiel. Just as the noting of the day on which the siege began was an implicit stress on the working of God, so the realization that the deprivation of the right of outward mourning had been foreseen and acted out would bring a consciousness that the destruction of city and sanctuary was an act of the sovereignty of God. But the realization of the sovereignty of God is the first step to a new hope (v. 24).

THE END OF EZEKIEL'S DUMBNESS (24: 25–27)

On p. 31 I discussed Ezekiel's "dumbness" in the context of 3: 26 without coming to any really certain conclusion. I did, however, consider that it was probably a symbolic dumbness, i.e. Ezekiel could speak normally, but refrained from doing so, except when he had a message to give from God. There is nothing in the explanation that does not fit the present context. "That day" (vv. 26f.) must not be stressed; it was not until six months after the destruction that a fugitive arrived with the news (see note on 33: 21, p. 118).

CHAPTER XII

THE PROPHECIES AGAINST THE NATIONS

THEIR PURPOSE

PROPHECIES against the nations are found in many of the prophetic books, most notably in Isaiah, Jeremiah and Ezekiel. With the exception of a very few, e.g. Isa. 18; Jer. 27: 1–11, it is most unlikely that the normal prophecy about the nations ever came to the ears of their rulers, and it is obvious that some were never intended to. The prophets' ministry was almost always to Israel, and if they spoke of Israel's neighbours, it was to enforce and explain their message to Israel.

There is no reason at all for thinking that Ezekiel's messages in these chapters were ever carried to the countries mentioned, and it is most improbable that they could have been. Their very position, which is that in Isaiah, and the original one in Jeremiah[1], points to their real purpose. The true Biblical teaching on the sovereignty of God is the mean between two extremes. We are apt so to stress the universal sovereignty of God and His judgments on the nations that do not know Him, that we are tempted to feel that there is room for some area of favouritism where His own people are concerned, that He can somewhat relax His requirements from them. A very large part of the prophetic message is devoted to disproving this idea, and this was the main purpose of Ezekiel's messages of judgment—that is one reason for their modern relevance. The opposite error is so to stress God's activities among His people, that we think of the nations as left to their own devices, and so we are tempted to despair when faced by their hostile forces. None of the exiles who had grasped and accepted Ezekiel's message were in danger of thinking that Jerusalem had fallen by accident, or because Jehovah was weaker than the gods of Babylon, but they were in very real danger of losing heart as they faced the gross darkness of heathendom around them. So to them was given this group of prophecies showing God's rule over and judgment on certain of the nations with whom they had been brought into contact.

[1] See my *Men Spake from God*, p. 77.

The nations dealt with fall into two obvious groups. First there are the Ammonites (25: 1–7), Moabites (25: 8–11), Edomites (25: 12–14) and Philistines (25: 15–17). Though, with the possible exception of the last, they had joined with Zedekiah in his plotting (Jer. 27: 2f.), they had made their peace with Nebuchadnezzar in time. They had then, as is so often the case, shown their loyalty by ostentatious zeal against Jerusalem. Ezekiel shows that their sudden shift in loyalties will not save them from their doom. The second group are Egypt (29–32) and Tyre (26: 1–28:19) with Sidon (28: 20–24). Here a symbolic element certainly enters in. Egypt is for Ezekiel the land where Israel learnt idolatry (20: 7f.) and trust in foreign powers (23: 3). Tyre represents the commerce of the time, rejected by more than one of the prophets as fundamentally evil and heartless. But, though I have never met any recognition of the fact, Tyre symbolizes Babylon itself, for all through its long history Babylon had been one of the greatest commercial centres of the world. Ezekiel could not foretell the downfall of Babylon without the most serious danger to him and his hearers. But if all Tyre's riches and commerce and the power that riches can buy could not save her in the hour of her need, then Babylon would equally go down to her fate, when her hour had struck. This must not be understood to imply that 26: 1–28: 19 are not really prophecies against Tyre. They are. If they were merely thinly veiled allegories, the Babylonians would have understood as well as Ezekiel's direct hearers. But for those that had ears to hear, the deeper meaning was present. This explains too why Ezekiel probably exaggerates the glory of Tyre, which had already begun to wane under the earlier attentions of the Assyrians.

A justification of this stress on the mercantile character of Babylon may be found partly in a reference to Ezekiel's own words in 16: 29 (see RV mg., RSV), 17:4. A few quotations from standard works will support it. "The Babylonians had a most modern idea of 'law and order,' and to this was no doubt due their commercial stability, which survived all wars and conquests unimpaired."[1] "The Assyrians, however, were not a commercial nation. . . . When the Babylonian merchants realized this, and saw that under the firm Assyrian rule of Northern Syria their trade was free from possible interference by the petty princes of that region . . . the merchants, the most important element in the body-politic, formed an unwavering pro-Assyrian party, which was ever ready to barter its self-

[1] Hall: *The Ancient History of the Near East*, p. 204.

respect for shekels."[1] "Commerical interests were therefore the leading influences in Babylonian life, even in religion." "Further, we must not lose sight of the fact that the Neo-Babylonian kings . . . engaged as freely in commercial trans-actions as the humblest of their subjects. At Babylon buying and selling and getting gain seen to have been in the very atmosphere of the place. This characteristic of the golden city appears to have continued long after her supremacy had passed away and to have furnished much of the imagery in Rev. 17."

THE PROPHECIES AGAINST ISRAEL'S NEIGHBOURS (25:1-17)

This group of prophecies creates few difficulties. They are very typical and are in many ways reminiscent of Amos 1:3-2:3. The accusation in each case fastens on one point, and the punishment is stated in fairly general terms. As we do not know enough details of the last hours of Jerusalem, we cannot fully appreciate the condemnations. It is interesting to note that v. 8 shows that Israel's claim to be Jehovah's elect people was already making it unpopular.

The doom prophesied against Ammon and Moab is that they should become the prey of Arab tribes. In fact it was not very long before their territory was occupied by the Nabateans. It is likely that "and Seir" (v. 8) should be omitted with the best MS. of LXX. "The side of Moab" (v. 9)—better "the shoulder of Moab"—is the long line of the mountains of Moab as seen from Jerusalem. The ICC with a small textual change renders the difficult words that follow "from Aroer in its whole extent."

The outstanding feature of the prophecy against Edom is that the ultimate instrument of punishment is to be Israel (v. 14). This was fulfilled in the time of John Hyrcanus (134-104 B.C.); he conquered the Edomites and gave them the choice of Judaism or the sword. Though many of the Edomites, or Idumeans, remembered their origin, they became fanatical Jews in reli-gion.[4] This was how Herod could become king of the Jews.

No agent of punishment is mentioned for the Philistines. In fact by the time of the Hashmoneans, i.e. after 165 B.C., the former Philistine cities regarded themselves as being Greek; the older elements in their population seem largely to have dis-appeared.

[1] Hall, *op. cit.*, p. 455.
[2] Breasted: *Ancient Times*, p. 174.
[3] Boutflower: *In and Around the Book of Daniel*, p. 138.
[4] Cf. Josephus: *Bel. Jud.* IV, iv-v.

THE CONDITIONAL NATURE OF PROPHECY

These prophecies introduce us to one of the major difficulties in Ezekiel, indeed in prophetic literature generally (cf. also pp. 52 and 132).

In ch. 26 he prophesies not merely the complete destruction of Tyre, but its destruction by Nebuchadnezzar. Moreover the destruction is to be final; Tyre will not be rebuilt (v. 14). Lest there should be any misunderstanding it is followed by a lament over Tyre (ch. 27), its prince (28: 1–10) and its king (28: 11–19). Yet sixteen years later—cf. 29: 17 with 26: 1—he announces that Nebuchadnezzar "had no wages from Tyre for the service that he served against it" (29: 18); in its place he promises him the spoil of Egypt (29: 19). In 30: 1–19 we have the prophecy of the results for Egypt. In 29: 1–16 is a description of the devastation of Egypt, which, however, is not directly linked with the promise to Nebuchadnezzar.

Tyre was besieged by Nebuchadnezzar from 856 to 573 B.C. and was terminated by Ithobaal the king acknowledging the supremacy of Babylon. In 567 B.C., the 37th year of Nebuchadnezzar, there was fighting between Babylon and Pharaoh Amasis, but unfortunately the tablet giving us the information is badly damaged and we cannot be sure whether Nebuchadnezzar penetrated into Egypt. The fact that he left inscriptions in the Isthmus of Suez certainly does not justify Petrie's dogmatic conclusion, "Thus he (Nebuchadnezzar) doubtless occupied the fortress of Tahpanhes" (cf. Jer. 43: 8–13).[1] All we can say from the available evidence is that Nebuchadnezzar will at the most have penetrated the border districts of the Delta, and may have fulfilled the Tahpanhes prophecy of Jeremiah, but certainly neither the wider prophecy of Jer. 43: 11ff. nor Ezek. 30: 1–19. Ezek. 29: 10–13 was not fulfilled either in the time of Nebuchadnezzar or later.

Tyre was taken and destroyed by Alexander the Great in 332 B.C., but only eighteen years later it had regained much of its earlier importance, which it was able to maintain to some extent right down to the time of the Crusades. After its recapture by the Saracens in 1291 it gradually dwindled into the fishing village it now is. It is argued by some that the prophecy of 26: 14 was in fact fulfilled, for it is claimed that Nebuchadnezzar did destroy the old town on the mainland, and that the city which was captured by Alexander and which carried on the name through the centuries was built on a small

[1] For the inscription see Pritchard: *Ancient Near Eastern Texts*, p. 308b, for Petrie's views his *Egypt and Israel*, p. 93, and for a general survey of the evidence, Hall: *The Ancient History of the Near East*, p. 549.

island off the original site.   The present village is also on this island site, though it has now been linked with the mainland by silting.   Even if we could consider that such a "fulfilment" were in fact an adequate meeting of the prophet's words, as if a slight shift in a town's site were to make it a new entity altogether, the suggestion is based on an error of fact.   It seems absolutely certain that the original town of Tyre was from the first on the island.   Whether it was also on the mainland, or whether that was a later extension is not clear, but the name given by the Greeks to the latter, Old Tyre, was due to misunderstanding.

It should be clear that the answer we give to this problem of unfulfilled prophecy will throw much light on the nature of the foretelling of the future as a whole.

Our starting point must be Jer. 18: 7–10.   Here it is stated categorically that all national prophecy is conditional.   It is based on conditions in existence at the time of the prophecy, and if these are changed, then the prophecy ceases to be in force. The most obvious example of this is Jonah's prophecy to Nineveh.   Not only was it not fulfilled, but quite obviously Jonah did not expect it to be (4: 2).

Except where a promise is confirmed by God's oath (Gen. 22: 16; Psa. 105: 9; Heb. 6: 13) we are safe in concluding that every statement of God about the future has some element of the conditional in it, something ancient Israel was as unwilling to believe as we are.   Where the prophecy is concerned mainly with the doom or prosperity of an individual or of a people, a change of behaviour can annul the prophecy.   This explains the apparent smugness of Hezekiah's answer to Isaiah (Isa. 39: 8), when the latter foretold the Babylonian captivity.   He knew that by living Godfearing lives his descendants could postpone the judgment indefinitely.   Something will have happened both in Tyre and in Egypt, and it may be in Babylon, to cause the doom uttered not to go into effect, and for Ezekiel this was so obvious that neither apology nor explanation was necessary.

Where, however, the prophecy is one of God's purposes of blessing to mankind, the element of condition is merely one of time and manner, not of substance.   For example, had David's successors walked in his ways, God's promise (II Sam. 7: 12–16) to David would have been fulfilled in all its details.   Their sin led to the fall of the royal house, but the essential portion of the promise was fulfilled in Christ.

If we could grasp this clearly, it would clear away much false exegesis on prophetic Scripture.   We would feel under no compulsion to explain away the obvious force of a promise like that of Huldah to Josiah (II Kings 22: 18ff.); many prophecies that are conveniently relegated to the Millennium, will be seen to refer to the time of the prophet; no difficulty will be found in recognizing minor contradictions and development in the message of any particular prophet.

This view may be challenged on the ground of general principle but this will not take us very far. The general principles of Scripture interpretation must be discovered in Scripture, not in our feeling of what is right and proper. Above all we can ignore the naïve complaint made to me that this deprives us of certainty *in details* in our study of prophecy yet unfulfilled; as though we were intended to have this certainty. Far more important is the challenge based on Daniel and Revelation, which give a very different picture to that suggested above. Not enough know that Daniel is not placed among the prophetic books in the Hebrew Canon of Scripture, and of those that know not sufficient take it seriously. When the modern scholar classes Daniel and Revelation as apocalyptic, it is no case of mere scholars' jargon. There is a deep difference between them and prophecy, as that term is normally understood in Scripture.

We are transported to that contradiction which runs through all Scripture, that between the sovereignty of God and the free-will of man. Prophecy appeals to the free-will of man. For that reason the absolute foreknowledge of God is veiled. An excellent example is to be found in Jer. 18: in v. 11 we have God's appeal to the people, which, if accepted, would invalidate so much that Jeremiah had foretold; yet in v. 12 is the clear indication that God knew well how the appeal would be received. God's foreknowledge and sovereignty never lead Him to ignore man's free-will, as He turns to plead with him. On the other hand apocalyptic reveals God's sovereignty. It is not God's appeal to man, but His encouragement of His own in the hour of their trial. There is no contingency in apocalyptic, but also, as the long history of exegesis shows, no certainty of interpretation. We have to choose in God's wisdom between the relative simplicity of prophecy with its contingency and the determinism of apocalyptic with its exegetical uncertainty.

Though I have said that prophecies of a nation's doom or blessing could be anulled, in most cases this is too strong a statement. Again and again where a prophecy was not fulfilled literally, we find it coming into force at a later date in all main essentials. Jonah did not see Nineveh destroyed, but about a century and a half later the Medes and Babylonians razed it to the ground, never to be rebuilt. Babylon in her turn was not destroyed in the manner prophesied by Jeremiah in ch. 50–51; but for all that Babylon sank in due course and did not rise again. Those that argue that Babylon must be rebuilt that it may be destroyed in accordance with prophecy have no strong ground to stand on.[1] Tyre was not destroyed by Nebuchadnezzar, and when it was destroyed two and a half centuries later, it was soon rebuilt. For all that the day came when it had sunk so low as a fishing village, that none that stand on the shore can imagine the old commercial centre in all its pride. Egypt was never left without inhabitant, but it has become "the basest of all kingdoms," and all the efforts of its politicians will never restore it to its old pre-eminence.

This very inadequate survey of this problem should show us once again that the foretelling of the future in prophecy has always a spiritual purpose, which is liable to be lost, if we concentrate on fulfilment. We have also been warned against reading preconceived ideas into Scripture, which must always be allowed to interpret itself.

THE DOOM OF TYRE (CH. 26)

In our study of Scripture we must beware of two contrasted errors. The expositor must never yield to the temptation of constantly striving for the new and the novel. On the other hand he must not allow himself to be unduly impressed by apparent unanimity of opinion on any one passage. It is generally agreed that "Aha, she is broken that was the gate of the peoples" (v. 2, RV) represents Tyre's rejoicing over the fall of a commercial rival, for "Caravan traffic from north to south would have been subject to taxation by the Jews" (NBC ad loc.).

Such an interpretation is doubly unacceptable. Even if we take Jerusalem as a personification of the kingdom of Judah, which is far from certain, it is very doubtful whether at any time after Solomon the southern kingdom had exercised any influence on the trade routes that were Tyre's concern. Josiah may possibly have had this power, but it will have been far too short a time to create the impression that Judah might become in any sense Tyre's rival. What is far more important is that Tyre's trade would be far more seriously threatened by Jerusalem's fall than by her continued existence. Once Babylon controlled the whole of the Mediterranean coast from the Taurus range to the frontier of Egypt it could exercise a stranglehold on Tyre's trade.

[1] This does not apply to those that base their view on their interpretation of Revelation.

The fundamental sin of Egypt was pride (29: 3, 9) that rendered it insensible to the needs of others (29: 6f.); the neighbours of Israel had been condemned for essentially spiritual sins (ch. 25), and at least in the case of Ammon (25: 3) and Moab (25: 8) it involved hatred of Israel's position and religion. It is reasonable to assume that the sin of Tyre was of the same type.

From whatever direction one approaches Jerusalem there is even today something about one's first view of it that stirs one's pulse. Partly it is due to the very unexpectedness of the city, among the bare hills of Judea. Though it is easy to exaggerate the unsuitability of its site for a capital, Jerusalem could never be a natural commercial centre. Even if the frontiers of the State of Israel were pushed to the Jordan or beyond it, Tel-Aviv would remain its commercial and industrial centre. The very reverse is true of Tyre. For the conditions of the time its position was ideal for world commerce. So too under very different surroundings was that of Babylon.

Both Isaiah (2: 2–4) and Micah (4: 1–4) had prophesied the day, when Jerusalem would be the magnet for all peoples. Jerusalem and Tyre stood for two goals, two ideals, two loyalties that could never be reconciled. It may well be, however, that the choice of the epithet "gate" is a cryptic pointer to the deeper meaning of the prophecy I suggested on p. 100. Babylon is really Babel, or Bab-ili, the Gate of God. It was not merely political or commercial supremacy that Babylon claimed, but religious too, as is reflected in Nebuchadnezzar's demand for the worship of the image of Marduk (Dan. 3: 1–6). The destruction of Jerusalem was a matter of joy to all forms of natural religion, especially those that glorified man's physical achievements.

C. S. Lewis in his *The Screwtape Letters* (p. 45) makes Screwtape say, "One must face . . . an appalling truth. He really *does* want to fill the universe with a lot of loathsome little replicas of Himself—creatures whose life, on its miniature scale, will be qualitatively like His own, not because He has absorbed them but because their wills freely conform to His. We want cattle who can finally become food; He wants servants who can finally become sons. We want to suck in, He wants to give out. We are empty and would be filled; He is full and flows over." Here is the difference between Tyre (or Babylon) and Jerusalem. But the many nations that Tyre looked to to replenish her shall be her doom (v. 3). Note in this connexion the rejoicing of the nations over the king of Babylon (Isa. 14: 9–20), and Jer. 51: 48.

Tyre's daughters (vv. 6, 8) are the suburbs of Tyre on the mainland. The isles (vv. 15, 18) are the more distant coastlands (so RSV in v. 15, but not v. 18), not necessarily islands, though they are included.

THE LAMENT OVER TYRE (CH. 27)

Ezekiel now compares Tyre to a gallant ship manned by sailors from the other Phoenician cities. It is caught in a storm and lost with all hands. It is lamented by sailors everywhere (vv. 3b–9a, 25b–36). Into this fine poem he has inserted a catalogue of Tyre's commerce in prose (vv. 9b–25a). This division is well seen in RSV though it erroneously reckons v. 9b as part of the poem.

The picture of Tyre as a ship was probably suggested by the fact that the city proper was an island; this explains v. 4a also. Senir=Hermon (v. 5; Deut. 3:9). Render v. 6b with RSV, "They made your deck of pines from the coasts of Cyprus, inlaid with ivory." Elishah (v. 7) has not been identified with certainty. Arvad (v. 8) was built on an island north of modern Tripoli. Since the ship is Tyre, there is much to be said for the conjecture that we should read Zemer in v. 8b (RSV, ICC, cf. Gen. 10:18), a town near Arvad. Gebal (v. 9) or Byblos = Jebeil between Beirut and Tripoli. Lud (v. 10) = Lydia; Put = Egyptian Punt, i.e. the African coast of Red Sea. "With thine army" (v. 11) should probably be "and Helech" = Cilicia (RSV, Moffatt); Gammadim—Gammad has not been identified with certainty. Tarshish (v. 12) here, by virtue of the metals mentioned, probably a Spanish town or district. Javan (v. 13) = Ionians; Tubal and Meshech, tribes from Asia Minor (see comment on 39: 1). Togarmah (v. 14) probably = Armenia. Dedan (v. 15) is mentioned again in v. 20 and so RSV, Moffatt, Cam. B., etc., follow LXX and render "the men of Rhodes"; ICC gives good reasons against and we may assume two branches of the Arab tribe, one in Edom, the other in Arabia. RSV, Moffatt, ICC follow 25 Hebrew MSS., Aquila and the implication of LXX and render Edom in v. 16; the difference is minimal, and the confusion has frequently been made in the Hebrew text. "Minnith . . . pannag" (v. 17) have had no certain explanation; the renderings of Moffatt and RSV are guesses. Helbon (v. 18) a famous vine-growing district N.E. of Damascus. The names in v. 19 have been corrupted, but no certain emendation has been offered. Though Canneh and Chilmad (v. 23) are presumably in Northern Mesopotamia, they have not been identified. Neither AV or RV of v. 25a can be said to be particularly intelligent; render with RSV, Moffatt, Cam. B., ICC, ". . . travelled for you with your merchandise."

"Suburbs" (v. 28) is misleading; "countryside" (RSV), or "coast" (Moffatt) is better. Similarly replace "astonished" (v. 35) by "appalled" (RSV, Moffatt). "Hiss" (v. 36): not a sound of disgust but of astonishment, cf. I Kings 9: 8.

The Downfall of the King of Tyre (28: 1–19)

This section contains a prophecy of the punishment of the king of Tyre (vv. 1–10) and a prophetic dirge over his fall (vv. 11–19). Many, contrasting *prince* (v. 2) with *king* (v. 12), think that two persons are intended, but this view is based on a misunderstanding.   Prince = *nagid*, which with varying English translation is a regular title for the Israelite kings, see especially I Sam. 9: 16; 10: 1, even though it is used for lesser men as well, for it means "leader."   It is deliberately used of the king of Tyre to stress that he only held his office at God's appointment.   King (*melek*) stresses the popular concept of kingship in the Fertile Crescent, which regarded the ruler as the representative of the gods and as more than human, though actual divinity was apparently only ascribed to him in Egypt.   In our exposition we shall see that the two titles are deliberately chosen to fit the contents of the two portions.

An Alleged Portrait of Satan

For many vv. 11–19 are primarily a picture of Satan, before his fall in a pre-Adamic Eden, looking forward to the Antichrist.[1]   Those who implicitly hold this view have generally little idea of how unknown it is in wider Christian circles, or of how little basis there is for it in fact.

The Jews "were intrusted with the oracles of God" (Rom. 3: 2).   There were deeper meanings in the Old Testament that could not be grasped until the Messiah came, but that is not the case here.   There were prophecies of Christ they refused to see once they had rejected Him, but that has no relevance here. Except in the two cases just mentioned it seems very hazardous to give to an Old Testament passage a meaning that Jewish exegesis knows nothing of.   In one very fanciful Rabbinic passage[2] it is said that the king of Tyre, incorrectly called Hiram, actually entered Paradise; otherwise they see the first man described in the passage.[3]

---

[1] The most careful exposition of this view known to me is in Pember: *Earth's Earliest Ages*, pp. 47–54 (15th edit.).

[2] *Derek Eretz Zuta* 1 at end.

[3] *Pesiqtha* 36b, 73b and six parallels in other works, *Wayyiqra Rabba* 20.

The application of the passage to Satan was common among leading Church fathers in the second half of the fourth century A.D. It is, however, striking that though it was held by Jerome, when he came to write his commentary on *Ezekiel* he omitted it.

Most cogent of all, however, is that any such interpretation detaches vv. 11–19 from their setting.   A striking feature of the book is its very real unity, but here we are asked to believe that without giving any warning Ezekiel's gaze wanders first back to a period before man, and then on to almost the end of time though apparently speaking of the contemporary scene.   The argument that much of the language could not be used of a mere man is really based on ignorance of the implications of Ezekiel's language.

It is worth mentioning that exactly the same arguments are valid against the efforts to interpret Isa. 14: 4–23 of the fall of Satan.   But this does not mean that there is no truth in the view.   All men who go the way of Satan mirror him and his sin in some measure.   There is a real parallel between the fall of proud man and proud tempter, but Scripture does not give a picture of the fall of Satan mirroring the fall of men, but the fall of men mirroring the yet greater fall of the evil one.

THE PRIDE OF THE KING OF TYRE (28: 1–10)

Ithobal II, king of Tyre, in spite of his pride, was merely Jehovah's *nagid*, the ruler He had appointed to lead Tyre, "for there is no power but of God" (Rom. 13: 1).   But in his own eyes he was a god (*'el*).   The use of *'el* rather than *'elohim* shows that he was not claiming deity, but rather that as representative of the gods he had been granted divine strength and power. Ezekiel tells him he is only *'adam* (v. 2), i.e. he is a man like all other men, linked with mankind for he is taken from one common soil (*'adamah*), to which, like all others, he will return.

Jeremiah had proclaimed to Ithobal among others (Jer. 27: 3) that Jehovah had set Nebuchadnezzar as king over him.   His defiance of the king of Babylon, based on the strength of Tyre (v. 2), was a defiance of Jehovah as well.   For Daniel (v. 3) see p. 59.   The heart of God (vv. 2, 6) is, of course, unchangeable. The plural "deaths" (vv. 8, 10) should be rendered "violent death."   The Phoenicians practised circumcision, while the Babylonians did not (v. 10), so not only would his vaunted power fail him, but he would fall by those he despised religiously (see also p. 115).

THE DIRGE OVER THE KING OF TYRE (28: 11–19)

Lamentation (v. 12) is a false translation of *qinah*, which means in itself a funeral dirge, the connotation of sorrow, which is inherent in lamentation, being secondary and indeed unnecessary.   Both here, and in 27: 2; 32: 2, 16; Amos 5: 1, sorrow is not implied but rather the opposite.   In the very similar passage, Isa. 14: 4–23, it is called a *mashal* (v. 4), i.e. a taunt-song. It has largely been this failure to realize the formal nature of *qinah*, the indubitable lack of sympathy in Ezekiel, and the traditional element of exaggeration in the average funeral dirge, that has prevented so many from recognizing the mockery in the prophet's words, which have then been taken literally.

In our justifiable rejection of the modern view that the early stories of Genesis are merely pagan myths purified of their polytheism we tend to forget the far truer view of our fathers that the pagan myths represent a polytheistic corruption of the truths of the Bible.   We do not know enough about Canaanite myth to be certain what form their corruption of the Eden story may have taken, but it is more than probable that we have it reflected here.   Many will find it distasteful to find it suggested that we may have heathen myth in the Bible, but they forget that, if I am right, we have here a mocking funeral dirge over a heathen king, in which a mocking use of the king's own beliefs is to be expected.

Adam was the first king; that is why the Messiah is "the second man" and "the last Adam."   In Israel the offices of king, priest and prophet were separated to show that human sin had brought in a dislocation in God's order that only the Messiah could heal.   But elsewhere the king was the re-embodiment of the first man, the perfect representative and vice-regent of the gods.[1]   It is this false proud view of the king of Tyre that Ezekiel is using.   If Ithobal is the re-embodiment of the first man, Ezekiel can speak of him as being in Eden—the different picture of Eden can be explained by supposing that it was so described in Canaanite myth.

Our detailed exposition of the dirge must cope with the difficulties of the Hebrew, which, as LXX suggests, are in large part due to an imperfectly transmitted text.   Though the force of v. 12 is clear enough, it is likely that the renderings of RSV, "You were the signet of perfection, full of wisdom and perfect in beauty," or Moffatt are nearer what Ezekiel said.   The nine precious stones of v. 13 reappear on the high priest's breast-

---

[1] See my *The Centrality of the Messianic Idea for the Old Testament* (Tyndale Press), pp. 9–14, and Bentzen: *King* and *Messiah*, ch. 5.

plate, so there is little doubt that LXX is correct in reading all twelve.

The crux in our understanding depends on the rendering of vv. 14, 16. The Hebrew is exceptionally difficult. When RSV renders, basing itself largely on LXX:

> With an anointed guardian cherub I placed you . . .
> I cast you as a profane thing from the mountain of God,
> and the guardian cherub drove you out
> from the midst of the stones of fire

it takes substantially the same course as Moffatt, ICC, Cam. B. and NBC. Ithobal-Adam is pictured all wise, the prototype priest, in Eden, which in the Canaanite myth was evidently placed on the mountain of the gods (v. 16). The first sin is transformed into Tyre's sin: "In the abundance of your trade you were filled with violence, and you sinned" (v. 16a, RSV).

Commentators find difficulty in "thy sanctuaries" in v. 18, for they do not see why Ezekiel should be concerned with heathen holy places. The difficulty was felt as early as LXX, which translated, "I have profaned." Equally unnecessary is Moffatt's "you have profaned your sacred position." The Hebrew prophets were fully aware that though the religion of their neighbours was false it yet contained broken elements of the truth. For them it was a grievous thing that any man should deliberately fall below what little of the truth might have been preserved for him.

THE DOOM OF SIDON (28: 20–23)

Sidon was almost certainly an older city than Tyre, indeed it was probably the oldest of the South Phoenician cities, cf. Gen. 10: 15. So, though by the time of David Tyre had become their chief city, the Phoenicians are called Zidonians, i.e. Sidonians, in the Old Testament, e.g. Judges 10: 12; 18: 7; I Kings 11: 1, 5; 16: 31; I Chron. 22: 4; Ezek. 32: 30. Tyre was so severely mauled by Nebuchadnezzar that under the Persians Sidon once more became the more important. This is probably the point of the oracle. Tyre had not come under the doom of God that others should profit by continuing in her ways. Sidon might seek to inherit Tyre's glory but would only share in her doom. Today Saida, as it is now called, is only a small port of purely local importance. "They shall know" (vv. 22, 23) hardly refers to the inhabitants of Sidon, but rather to the survivors of Israel.

THE RESTORATION OF ISRAEL (28: 24–26)

Though Egypt was technically the neighbour of Israel, the sand-sea between them was a very effective barrier. Since the invasion of Shishak (I Kings 14: 25f.) and Zerah (II Chron. 14: 9–15)[1] Egypt had played little part in Judah's history beyond using her as a cat's-paw to protect herself against Assyria and Babylon. Both Isaiah (Isa. 30: 7) and the Rabshakeh (II Kings 18: 21) had mocked her ineffective show of strength. So before turning to the old crocodile of the Nile Ezekiel here sums up God's condemnation of Israel's true neighbours, big and little, that had harmed her. He indicates clearly that all are covered, whether they have been mentioned by name or not. This short oracle is a preparation for ch. 33–39.

It is worth noting that God will bring Israel to know Him along a twofold road. "Ye (they) shall know that I am Jehovah" occurs in slightly variant forms fifty-four times in Ezekiel (see p. 37). It never refers to any subjective, intuitive or mystic knowledge of God, but to the learning of His character by His works of judgment. But these works of judgment are equally on apostate Judah and on the God-defying nations; on the nations they are purely judgment, but on His people their ultimate object is grace.

THE PROPHECIES AGAINST EGYPT (CH. 29–32)

We have here a group of seven prophecies: 29: 1–16 is dated about January 587 B.C., some seven months before the fall of Jerusalem; there is every reason for thinking that 30: 1–19 is from approximately the same time; 30: 20–26 is dated about April 587 B.C. and 31: 1–18 is two months later, little over a month before the fall of the city; 32: 1–16 and 32: 17–32 were spoken within a fortnight of one another early in 585 B.C., i.e. after the fall of Jerusalem; finally 29: 17–21, the latest dated prophecy in the book, comes on New Year's Day, 571 B.C.—its position is explained by its being in some measure an expansion of 29: 1–16.

That numbers are used symbolically in Scripture, and especially in a book like Ezekiel, is obvious, and none is more often so used than seven. Yet here only preconceived ideas are likely to find any symbolical significance in the seven prophecies for surely 29: 17–21 was not added just to make up the seven. The more we became acquainted with the revelation of God, the more we gain the impression of supreme common sense, if we

---

[1] If he was an Egyptian; see NBC, p. 357b.

may reverently use this term of God. The Scriptures obstinately refuse to fit into any human prefabricated mould, and repeatedly the obvious and simple interpretation is the correct one.

THE DOOM OF EGYPT (29: 1-16)

We have here an allegorical poem (vv. 3ff., cf. RSV) and its prose interpretation. Pharaoh is compared to a water monster (*tannin*), i.e. a crocodile. There is nothing to be said for the traditional rendering "dragon." There is a deeper meaning as well. *Tannin* is used as a parallel to Leviathan in Isa. 27: 1 and to Rahab—used of Egypt in Isa. 30: 7, RV—in Isa. 51: 9. The comparison is not only with the ugly, complacent head of the crocodile protruding from the waters of the Nile, but also with the old rebellious chaos powers that Semitic mythology spoke of. Pharaoh's subjects are compared to the fish of the Nile.

Two reasons are given for Pharaoh's punishment, but it is likely that both ultimately go back to the same cause.

The lesser is his completely callous use of Israel as a cat's-paw (vv. 6f.). This was clearly seen by the Rabshakeh (II Kings 18: 21), and it lies behind Isaiah's condemnation of every approach to and entanglement with Egypt (see also p. 64). Behind the Pharaoh's willingness to use others without any thought of their welfare lay not only the natural selfishness of man but even more the belief that he was a god incarnate. It is always a very evil thing when a man persuades himself that for any reason he is not subject to the normal limitations of man; he will always end by falling lower than the normal level of mankind.

The greater cause of punishment was Pharaoh's pride, a pride that will have gone back to the same origin. His claim, "My Nile is my own; I have made it" (v. 3, RSV) was peculiarly foolish. The Nile is the life of Egypt; on its mysterious rise and fall depends the fertility and life of the land. One could almost say that the Nile is Egypt. But whether Egypt's southern frontier was the normal one of the First Cataract at Syene (Aswan), or whether at the height of Egypt's power it was moved a thousand miles upstream to the Sixth Cataract south of Meroe, the sources of the Nile and the mystery of its flooding that meant life for Egypt remained unknown, as Herodotus bears testimony. Then and now man's ability to use the forces of nature leads him to believe that he is lord of nature and that he can dispense with its true Lord.

The punishment of Egypt is conquest ("a sword", v. 8), for

it had callously given up others to conquest, and the failure of
the Nile floods ("an utter waste and desolation," v. 10, 30: 12)
from the Delta to the First Cataract—from Migdol to Syene
(v. 10, RV mg., RSV). Though the complete desolation for
forty years (vv. 11ff.) has seen no literal fulfilment, nor is there
the slightest reason to think that it will, Egypt has seen
repeated conquest, famine and humiliation. Modern Egypt
dreams of a renewal of past glories, but we may be sure that
any apparent satisfaction will be of short duration.

Egypt's Humiliation (29: 17 – 32: 16)

In God's wisdom, whatever blows Egypt may have suffered
from Nebuchadnezzar, and however far he may have penetrated
across the frontier, he was not the executor of God's wrath.   It
may be that there were spiritual reasons in Egypt; it may be
that it was Nebuchadnezzar's pride, so graphically described in
Daniel, that deprived him of this conquest, which was reserved
for Cambyses, the son of Cyrus (525 B.C.).   It would have been
more merciful for Egypt had Persia been able to keep a firm
grip on the land.   It was ruined by constant fighting and brutal
extortion, so that the conquest by Alexander the Great in
332 B.C. was hailed with joy.   There followed the long line of
fifteen Ptolemys, Greeks by blood, culture and outlook.   Under
them Egypt became, at least in its cities, and to some measure
even in the countryside, Hellenized.   The alien royal house
degenerated more and more until after the battle of Actium it
dropped like a ripe plum into the hands of the Romans in 30 B.C.

Since then it has been ruled by Arab and Turk, Fatimid and
Saracen, Mamluk, Ottoman, Turk and Albanian.   Misrule,
extortion and plague have kept the land poor.   Even its language has disappeared, displaced first by Greek and then by
Arabic, leaving only "the mere jargon"[1] of ecclesiastical Coptic.
Even were Egypt to rise once again to the rank of a first-class
state, it would be no more a true descendant of the Egypt that
once was than is modern Italy of ancient Rome, or Greece of
Athens and Sparta.

In his valuable study of ch. 27[2] Prof. Sidney Smith suggests
that the reason why Nebuchadnezzar gained no wealth, when
he finally captured Tyre (29: 18), was that as he could not
invest it by sea, its riches were shipped off, either for necessities
or safety, during the siege, and he explains 27: 27, 34, in this
way.   "Every head was made bald, and every shoulder was

---

[1] *Chambers's Encyclopaedia*, Vol. V, p. 32b.

[2] *The Ship Tyre* in *Palestine Exploration Fund Quarterly*, 1953, p. 97 seq.

peeled" ("rubbed bare," RSV) in Nebuchadnezzar's army
(29: 18) by the constant wearing of helmets and the carrying
of burdens for the siege works.

EGYPT IN SHEOL (32: 17–32)

As this section is appealed to by various smaller sects as a
justification for their views on "life" after death, it calls for
somewhat closer attention.

It is clear that vv. 19–21 are a funeral dirge over Egypt;
whether vv. 22–32 are also in poetry or only in rhythmic prose
must with our present knowledge remain doubtful.   The doubt
arises, as in certain other poetic passages in Ezekiel, from the
uncertain state of the text.   In either case, however, we are
dealing, as in Isa. 14: 4–21 with poetic language and imagery,
and it is inadvisable to take all the details literally.

Ezekiel is called to seal Pharaoh's fate by taking up the
funeral dirge (v. 18, cf. 27: 2; 28: 12 and see p. 32) in which
he is to be joined by representatives of the nations—read, "send
them down with a lament, you and the women of the mighty
nations" (Moffatt).   The versions bear testimony to the uncertainty of the text in v. 20.   The RSV, "They shall fall amid
those who are slain by the sword, and with her shall lie all her
multitudes," is attractive but not certain.   Just as in Isa.
14: 9f. the great chiefs among the dead in Sheol greet the dead
Pharaoh (vv. 19, 21).

Ezekiel then pictures Pharaoh touring Sheol.   He sees each
nation with its own portion.   Assyria, Elam, etc., represent in
each case the king and around him lie the bodies of his warriors.
On the basis of this it has been claimed that Sheol is no more
than a poetic name for the grave; it should be clear, however,
that here we are dealing entirely with poetic and semi-symbolic
imagery.   In the first place the kings of each nation are represented by one typical figure, possibly, in the setting, the last
of his line.   Then his warriors are buried around him as they
never were in fact, especially when their kingdom went down
in fire and storm.   The weapons in v. 27 are as much shadow
weapons as everything else in Sheol.   The fact is that Sheol is
so much a shadow land, that so far as reality for the living is
concerned, it matters not whether its inhabitants are pictured
as rising to greet the newcomer in irony, or whether they are
seen tidily taking their rest, each in his appointed place.

Already in 28: 10 we had the death of the uncircumcised as
a mark of shame; here it is virtually a refrain.   In the setting
Moffatt's "a shameful death" seems to bring out the meaning best.

One of the vexed questions in the Old Testament is whether it recognizes any difference of position among the dead, any divisions of Sheol. Terms like "the uttermost parts of the pit" (v. 23) can hardly be made to bear any such construction by themselves, and the general impression we gain is that there is no discrimination in Sheol. But what are we to make of v. 27? It certainly suggests discrimination and difference. On the whole, however, though neither Moffatt nor RSV agree, it seems best to follow LXX and Syriac with most modern commentaries and omit the negative. No reason seems to be given or suggested for differentiating between Meshech-Tubal and the "mighty men of old" (so RSV, Moffatt following the Versions), and probably none is intended. Equally we should probably follow recent commentators, and also RSV, Moffatt, in the conjectural reading involving a very small consonantal change "whose shields are upon their bones" instead of "their iniquities are upon their bones."

Meshech-Tubal, as the concord "her" shows, is a compound name (as against RSV and Moffatt). Though the commentators think of tribes in Asia Minor, as is indeed the case in 27: 13, it seems unlikely here. There is no evidence that the difficulties the Muski created for the Assyrians through the centuries had made any great mark on Judah's memory, nor does the interpretation explain the compound name, which many commentators seek to avoid by omitting Tubal. It seems far more likely that the names are used as in 39: 1 (see p. 134) of the wild tribes that periodically broke into the Fertile Crescent, coming no one knew from where. The most recent example had been the Scythians, who had appeared suddenly round the end of the Caucasus, had rocked Assyria to its foundations and had been virtually exterminated by the Medes.

Though the Edomites and the Phoenicians had not yet gone down to Sheol, the word of the Lord had gone out against them, and so with prophetic certainty they are included in the picture. "The princes of the north" are the petty kings of Northern Syria.

So Pharaoh is left with the cold comfort (v. 31) that as is the doom of all nations that forget God so was his—for Ezekiel's hearers there was the further message, clear even if unexpressed, that as Egypt had gone, so would Babylon go in the day of God's choice. It is hard to imagine a more dramatic close to Ezekiel's prophecies against the nations. He now turns to the future of Israel; the destruction of Jerusalem can be followed by national resurrection, but there is no future for the nations of the world as they go down into silence.

CHAPTER XIII

PROPHECIES OF RESTORATION

WHILE Ezekiel waited anxiously for news from besieged Jerusalem, news that he knew could only be of destruction, God re-commissioned him, for now a new phase of work was to begin. Whereas he had previously been primarily a messenger of doom, he was now to be the builder of a new community.

Whether there was a new vision of the chariot-throne we are not told. It does not matter, but probably there was not. Visions and ecstatic experiences belong mostly to the beginnings of communion with God. There are those that measure spirituality by such measuring rods, but in fact they are very often God's compensation for its lack. When a man has walked with God for six years, as had Ezekiel, he does not need visions to guarantee the source and authority of the voice that spoke to him.

Vv. 2–9 are essentially the same as 3: 17–21 (see p. 29), but with two important differences. The parallel between Ezekiel and a watchman is more fully drawn (vv. 2–6). This reflects Ezekiel's changed status in the community. As the storm clouds gathered over Jerusalem he had increasingly been winning the ear and the regard of the exiles; when his message was vindicated by the fall of Jerusalem, he would become an undisputed spiritual leader. So we are given both the human and the divine side of his appointing.

On the other hand the danger to the righteous is not mentioned (cf. 3: 20f.). This had been above all despondency, lack of trust and a following of those false voices that had whispered spurious hopes of speedy return from exile and a restoration of the glories of Zion. If in spite of all they had listened to and believed Ezekiel's message, its fulfilment would remove their chief danger. On the other hand, the wicked, for whom the pull of the surrounding heathendom was perhaps the chief danger, would feel themselves drawn by it the more now that the temple was no more and the enemies of Jehovah seemed to have triumphed.

The second part of the commissioning (vv. 10–20) is a summary of ch. 18 (see pp. 71–75), though again with a shift of emphasis.   Then the temptation had been for the exiles to see themselves so caught up by the entail of the past that effort on their part was useless.   Now, as with dull foreboding they waited for the end of all hope, their fate seemed so evil that the doing of God's will seemed to offer no hope of improving it.

Earlier Ezekiel had to bring home to the exiles that their very exile was an act of God's grace; now he had to make them see that their share in the future, their living, would depend entirely on their loyalty to God.   They could not lift the burden of exile, nor does Ekekiel suggest that it might be ameliorated. But under a harsh and capricious government their very survival was in itself a guarantee of a fulfilment of the promises of return.

The Church has known its Babylonian Captivity, and those that pass through it are tempted to conformity with the corrupt systems around it.   But whether in the dark night of medieval superstition or in the shorter persecutions of later days God has always preserved a handful of the faithful; their very living has been the best guarantee that the truth would some day triumph again.

"The City is Smitten!" (33:21–33)

Some six months after the fall of Jerusalem (cf. v. 21 with II Kings 25:3f.) the long expected news came.   It is imperative to read "eleventh" in v. 21 with eight Hebrew MSS., some MSS. of LXX and the Syriac, unless we assume, as does ICC (*ad loc.*), that a double system of time-reckoning is involved. In any case it must be August 586 B.C. that is intended, for while the fugitive could indeed have met many difficulties and delays on the road, Nebuchadnezzar's official dispatch must have been known in Babylon long before the year was out, and the gloating of minor officials and insolent neighbours would have brought them the news, even if it had not been conveyed officially.

Ezekiel had known it already the day before (v. 22), and with the knowledge came the release from his dumbness.   If my explanation of this is correct (pp. 31 and 98), it means that Ezekiel was now free to act as a normal teacher among the people and to enter into all the details of their lives.   This seems supported by the impression given by ch. 34–39 that they are merely a summary of a much fuller teaching.   Note that we are given no time indication in these chapters.

But before we are given the new message we have a double picture of the people that are left.   In vv. 24–29 we have a glimpse of the unrepentant remnant in Judea. Jer. 40–43 gives us a fuller picture of them and shows at least part of the fulfilment of the prophecy. There is a religious fanaticism that nothing can shake. We saw in Ezekiel's earlier prophecies the blind confidence of the men who believed that the temple could not be destroyed (cf. Jer. 7: 4) and that it would guarantee their safety. Now they had switched their confidence from the temple to their origin (v. 24). In a time of anarchy their behaviour had only deteriorated (vv. 25f.)—"ye stand upon your sword," i.e. you live by violence.

As for the exiles (vv. 30–33), Ezekiel had now become the topic of general conversation—the AV "against thee" (v. 30, see mg.) is particularly unfortunate. He was the popular preacher and the craze for the moment (v. 31). With the disappearance of Jerusalem as a centre of possible rebellion the position of the exiles improved greatly. The new possibilities of gain (v. 31, RV, RSV) were so filling their thoughts that the message of restoration had little attraction for them, and it would need the fulfilment of Ezekiel's new message before they would take him really seriously in his new role (v. 33).

RULERS PAST AND FUTURE (CH. 34)

In a day when monarchy is a convenience and a nostalgic inheritance from the past, we find it very hard to understand the role of the king in the Bible. Throughout the Bible lands monarchy was a divine institution; the king was the gods' supreme representative, himself a god in Egypt, a man capable of achieving deity elsewhere—chief ruler, chief priest, chief prophet. Though in Israel this union of offices was dissolved, a psalm like 110 shows that men looked for the Messianic king that would reunite them.[1] It followed that a people who were living out the will of Jehovah would have to have a head who truly represented Him. So in his picture of restored Israel Ezekiel begins with a picture of the king, though, as the prophecy develops, a deeper reason for this becomes apparent.

One of the disadvantages of fallen man is his very great difficulty, if not incapability, in picturing the ideal and perfect described purely in terms of itself. It is only when we see it against the background of the imperfect that we can really appreciate it. Hence Ezekiel begins with a picture of the kings as they had been (vv. 2–8).

Ezekiel uses the metaphorical name "shepherd." It cannot

[1] See my *The Centrality of the Messianic Idea for the Old Testament*, pp. 9–14.

be too emphatically stressed that whenever shepherd is used metaphorically it means king, except in the comparatively rare cases where the context makes it clear that the highest princes of the land are intended. The term is used especially by writers round the exilic period, e.g. Jeremiah and Zechariah, and was probably chosen to rule out the illegitimate religious connotations that had become attached to "king" (*melek*). When the title is used of God, it thinks of Him as the perfect king, Psa. 23: 1, etc.

At the same time it was peculiarly suited to stress the royal duty of enforcing social righteousness. ICC considers that Josiah's successors are here intended, but I think that the whole monarchy is under condemnation. Ezekiel's eye can see the rottenness under the surface, where we may be dazzled by superficial appearances, cf. his root and branch condemnation of Israel's religious history (ch. 20). Already in our study of 22: 30 (p. 91) we had reason to find a far-reaching condemnation of the kings. It is by examining the social record of the better kings that we can best see how little the monarchy had provided true shepherds for God's people.

I Sam. 8: 11–18 gives a prophetic preview of the social effects of the monarchy. We know too little of Saul's reign to be able to say how far he conformed to the pattern, though there are indications, e.g. I Sam. 22: 2; 25: 10 that the process had begun. II Sam. 20: 24 shows that David had already begun the hated system of "forced labour" (RSV; "levy," RV mg.), how hated may be seen from I Kings 12: 18. The cry for less taxation and forced labour (I Kings 12: 4) shows there was a side to Solomon's glory we often tend to forget. The evidence heaps up when we come to the written prophets. Isa. 5: 8–24 can be dated with reasonable certainty in the reign of Jotham (cf. II Kings 15: 34) and Mic. 2: 1–11; 3: 1–12 in that of Hezekiah (cf. Jer. 26: 18). Equally certainly Jer. 5 and Hab. 1: 2–4 belong to Josiah's reign *after* his reformation. It is noteworthy that the fullest picture of the Messianic king (Isa. 11: 1–9) stresses virtually only that he is the creator and maintainer of social righteousness.

We need not doubt that the religiously better kings were also socially better, but all of them failed to see that they were trying to make the best of a fundamentally evil system. There is no evidence that they ever even considered the possibility of placing the monarchy on any other basis than that foretold by Samuel.

The past rises so vividly before Ezekiel's eyes that he can speak of the vanished kings in the present tense (vv. 2ff.); in

vv. 5f. we have a reference to the exile. Then in vv. 7–10 he tells the royal family that restoration of national life will not bring the restoration of their privileged position with it. This is more than merely barring Jehoiachin's descendants from the throne. This had already been done by Jeremiah (22: 30). Ezekiel goes further. Instead of announcing the accession of a collateral branch of the Davidic family, or even of a new dynasty, he proclaims that for the time being Jehovah Himself would be their king with no man as His representative (vv. 11–16).

How remarkable the fulfilment has been. Under the long centuries of Persian and Greek rule (538–142 B.C.) there was no official head of the Jewish people, although increasingly the high priest was looked on as such, but his position was one of respect rather than of right. When in 140 B.C. the people regularized the existing position, they gave to Simon the Hashmonean the position of "leader and high priest for ever, until there should arise a faithful prophet; and that he should be captain over them, and should take charge of the sanctuary, to set them over their works, and over the country, and over the arms, and over the strongholds . . ." (I Macc. 14: 41f.). Apparently no king from the house of David was proposed, but on the other hand the title king was carefully withheld from Simon, for the people knew they had no right to bestow it.

When Simon's son, John Hyrcanus, assumed the royal title,[1] it meant a bitter breach between him and the Pharisees. The Hashmonean priest-kings fell in 63 B.C. only to be followed by the half Edomite Herods, whose only claim to the throne was the power of the Roman sword behind them. It was more than mere hatred of the Herodian family that prompted the embassage of Jewish notables to Rome after the death of Herod the Great (4 B.C.) asking that Palestine might be incorporated in the Roman province of Syria instead of a new king being appointed over them.[2] They had accepted the principle that only a king of God's appointing could really be a blessing to them.

The object of Jehovah's shepherding was to be the reformation of His people (vv. 17–22). The meaning will become clearer, if we substitute "sheep" for "cattle" in vv. 17, 20, 22; the rams and the he-goats are, of course, the rich and powerful among the people. All those who abuse the power of rank and wealth are to experience the judgment of God. We are apt to

---

[1] Josephus (*Ant.* XIII. xi. 1) affirms that Aristobulus, Hyrcanus' son, was the first to assume the royal title, but modern scholars are in agreement that Hyrcanus must already have done so.

[2] Josephus: *Ant.* XVII. xi. 2.

overlook the reality of God's working in Israel through the long centuries of his hardening in part. We doubt that any other nation can parallel the Jews' centuries' long rule by the wisest, by spiritual leaders. Probably no other people in the world to-day has a truer understanding of democracy or has less real class distinction. By centuries of suffering they have largely learnt the limitations of purely physical power, and the well-known generosity of the Jew shows that he has often understood the true purpose of wealth. Obviously there are many Jews that do not live up to their national ideals, and there are faults they are prone to which may be less common among the peoples in whose midst they live. For all that the objection of the Jew to the Church—quite apart from the way he has been treated by it—that he finds more understanding for social righteousness in the Synagogue than in the Church is, alas, all too often justified.

When Jehovah's purpose with His flock is accomplished, He appoints His "servant David" king over them (vv. 23–31). It is true he is called prince (*nasi*'), but, as 37:24f. show, this is not intended to deny that he is king. This is not the usage of 12: 10 and 21: 25 (cf. pp. 51 and 86). Here, and in 44: 3; 45: 7; 46: 2, the use of *nasi*' is meant to stress that God's king will not obscure the kingship of God; he will represent, not misrepresent Him. "My servant David" implies both the fulfilment of the promises of God to David and also that "Great David's greater Son" would truly be a man after God's own heart. There is general agreement that we should read with LXX in v. 31, "You are My sheep, the sheep of My pasture."

THE DOOM OF THOSE THAT HATE ISRAEL (CH. 35)

It is usually taken for granted that we have here merely one more prophecy against Edom, but a little thought will show us that, as so often, the apparently obvious can do with recon-sideration. The punishment of Edom was already announced in 25: 12–14, its natural position, and in 36: 5 Edom receives special mention among the lands coveting the soil of Israel. Unless we assume, in spite of the lack of any positive evidence, that Edom had already begun its infiltration into the Negeb that was to bring it as far as Hebron by the time of Judah's return, there seems no adequate spiritual motivation for this added denunciation. We have, however, seen that the pro-phecies against Egypt and Tyre (cf. pp. 113 and 105) have a deeper purpose than the superficial and obvious one, and we may well examine whether the same is not true here.

The first thing that should strike us in the unusual name, Mount Seir, which Ezekiel uses for Edom. It is found nowhere else in his prophecies—it was pointed out on p. 101 that the not completely parallel "Seir" in 25: 8 is probably due to textual corruption—its use in the Old Testament is comparatively rare, and except in this chapter it is a purely geographical expression. Since it is Ezekiel we are studying, we cannot go far wrong, if we look for a symbolic meaning.

Esau's "blessing" was, "Away from the fatness of the earth shall be thy dwelling, and away from the dew of heaven from above" (Gen. 27: 39, RV mg., RSV, etc.), and nothing symbolized this better than Mt. Seir. G. A. Smith describes it: "Few territories of this size cover such a range of soils. In parts well-watered, in others with a precarious agriculture, the most is unproductive. . . . Mount Esau [i.e. Mt. Seir] attains a general elevation of 4,000 to 5,000 feet above sea-level, far higher than that of Hauran, Gilead, or Moab . . . the variety of Mount Esau is thus greater than that of the Range to the north. Besides the cool stony plateaus, which it has like the latter but lifts higher, its west flank is a series of ridges, shelves and strips of valley, mazes of peaks, cliffs, and chasms that form some of the wildest rock scenery in the world. In the sandstone above the Arabah are the Siks (shafts), clefts or corridors between perpendicular rocks. Springs emerge between the porous upper strata of limestone and at the contact of the latter with the sandstone. On the limestone plateau devoid of springs cisterns preserve some of the winter rain, and at various periods dams and reservoirs have caught the surface waters in both the shallow and deep wadies."[1]

Mt. Seir may indeed act as a symbol of the lot of all those who despise their birthright and set as their goal "the lust of the flesh, and the lust of the eyes, and the vainglory of life." Their achievement may at first sight excite admiration and even envy, but at its latter end it is sterile.

From the time of Amos Edom is charged with implacable hatred against Israel (Amos 1: 11; Ezek. 25: 12; 35: 5; Obad. 10; Psa. 137: 7). The fact that we can so easily understand this hatred in no way diminishes their sin. The long periods of subjection to Judah, and the cruelty of Joab (I Kings 11: 15f.), in itself probably a reply to treachery, may palliate their hatred but do not excuse it in God's eyes. None hate the people of God, be it the Church or be it Israel, more than those that have despised God's giving in grace and have seen their own achievements prove sterile and empty. It was a true instinct that

---

[1] *The Historical Geography of the Holy Land*, 25th edit., p. 561–565.

made the rabbis apply the name Edom to Rome with all its pomp and spiritual emptiness.

So before Ezekiel turns to the accomplishment of God's purpose with His land and people, he solemnly foretells judgment on all those, who having gone their own way like Edom, hate the people of God and seek to deprive them of what is theirs by God's giving.

Note v. 10. Though Jehovah had abandoned His land (11: 23), that was something merely apparent and external. What has been chosen in God's election remains eternally His (cf. Rom. 11: 1f., 28f.).

RESTORATION: OUTWARD AND INWARD (CH. 36)

Ezekiel's message of restoration began with the monarchy (ch. 34), for without leadership chosen by God and well-pleasing to Him the people cannot prosper. After a digression dealing with those that hate God's people, Ezekiel turns not, as we might expect, to a transformed people, but to their transformed land. Since we are dealing here with a concept strange to the modern man, we will do well to examine it more closely.

THE TRANSFORMED LAND (36: 1–15)

For the average modern man a juxtaposition of land and people in a spiritual setting is meaningless. As a result this section is normally spiritualized away or used as yet another example of the material and inferior character of the Old Covenant. We shall see that though this attitude is not altogether unjustified, it fails to do justice to Scripture and exposes those that adopt it to very real spiritual danger.

For the Bible man is essentially material. He is 'adam, for he is made of the dust of the 'adamah (cf. in a different setting, p. 72). The solidarity of mankind lies not, as in Greek thought, in his being partaker of one spirit but of one body-stuff. It is his individuality that is guaranteed by the spirit breathed into him, which makes him personally answerable to God. So a man and the land on which he lives and from which he draws his nourishment are linked, and he by his sin can bring a curse on it, cf. 36: 17; Deut. 24: 4; Jer. 3: 1, 9; Psa. 106: 38; 107: 34. The Old Testament ideal is that a man should have his ancestral portion of land, which thanks to the law of Jubilee could not be permanently alienated (Lev. 25). Passages like Deut. 8: 7–9; 11: 10–12 hardly imply that

Palestine is the fairest of lands, but rather that it is the land of God's perfect choice for Israel.

The New Testament neither denies nor abrogates this basic truth about man's being. It does not preach a pale internationalism of the type so popular in socialist movements today, but it lifts the Christian, not mankind, to a new level. "Our citizenship is in heaven" (Phil. 3: 20, RV—Moffatt expresses the sense excellently by, "We are a colony of heaven"), where in a spiritual sense we already are (Col. 3: 1; Eph. 1: 3; 2: 6); we draw our sustenance from the body and blood of the new Adam, who is not earthy but is "the Lord from heaven." Therefore we have been lifted above questions of Jew and Gentile to become the Church of God (I Cor. 10: 32). It is only in measure as the Church and the individual Christian are lifted to a truly supernatural and spiritual plane that it can ignore the great basic verities of human nature. Much of the greatest tragedy in the Church comes, when its members living on a more or less material and natural plane attempt that which only the spiritual can do in fear and trembling.

There is a growing understanding in widening circles today that much of our modern malaise is due to man's divorce from the land and to the artificial conditions of city life. Modern man in his pride constantly wishes to defy the laws of his being, but nature always has the last word.

The Church cannot hope for perfection until our Lord Jesus comes from heaven as a Saviour to take it there; equally the transformation of Israel on the earthly level must be preceded by the transformation of the land.

In ch. 6 Ezekiel had denounced the mountains of Israel, because of the idolatry that had been carried out on them and which had defiled them. For that reason the message of transformation is addressed to them too. But there is a further complex of ideas why they are singled out for mention. Though the whole land had been given Israel by God, fear of the walled towns and the iron chariots had delayed the capture of the plains; the Philistine lands in the south of the Coastal Plain became tributary in the time of David, but already under Solomon they had once again become independent not again to come under Israelite rule until the time of the Hashmonean kings. It is very possible for men so to fail to possess their spiritual possessions that in the end they make excuses for not possessing them and persuade themselves that they are not intended to have them. It is a commonplace among Christians, for example, to deny the possibility of true holiness in this life, or to affirm that certain gifts of the Holy Spirit were only

intended for the first days of the Church.   In 47: 13–20 it is
clear that God's original giving holds good, but here Ezekiel
speaks in terms of that to which men had grown familiar.   We
can, however, legitimately consider the plains of Palestine to be
included in the language of ch. 36.   Whether one stands in the
Coastal Plain or in Esdraelon, one is more conscious of the hills
than of the plain; it is they that set the predominant note,
hence the description in Deut. 11: 11.

For the right understanding of vv. 4–6 we must bear in mind
that Ezekiel is not speaking of Judah only but of Israel as well,
where strangers had ruled for over a century and a half.   The
clear implication of vv. 9–11 is that the new settlers had been
unable to derive full profit from the soil.   There are many
natural explanations, all of which are superficially valid, why
Palestine has never been a truly fertile land for long ever since
Israel was driven out.   God uses natural means for accom-
plishing His purposes.   The wit of man may do what it will, but
God sees to it that the land of His choice does not show its true
riches until it is once again linked to the people of His choice.
In the last analysis Deut. 11: 12 remains true—Palestine will
always be what God makes it, not what man tries to make of it.

The translation "high places" (v. 2) is misleading; RSV "the
ancient heights" is preferable; the prophet uses *bamot* in its non-
technical sense, but allows the hearer to remember the misuse
of the hill-tops as sanctuaries.

Already in the story of the spies (Num. 13: 32) we are told
that Canaan is "a land that eateth up the inhabitants thereof."
We are presumably to understand this in a double sense.   The
position of Palestine is such that it has at all times been
exposed to invasion both from major powers in the Near East
and from the constant inroads and infiltration of the nomad
tribes in the east.   The traditional lists of pre-Israelite peoples
(Gen. 15: 19ff., etc.) show how from the earliest times this process
was going on.   Then too it has always been a land where the
risk of inadequate rainfall, locust swarms, pestilence from Egypt
and other natural catastrophes has made life precarious.   Now
all this is to be no more (vv. 12–15); Jehovah's presence (48: 35)
will preserve from both dangers.

THE TRANSFORMED PEOPLE (36: 16–38)

A belief in his own merit, or in his ability to acquire merit
with God is one of man's commonest and most subtle sins.
Ezekiel's stress that the exiles under Jehoiachin had been
peculiarly the recipients of God's grace will, after the fulfilment

of God's judgment on Jerusalem, have convinced many of them that in some way they had merited God's choice of them. Ezekiel is therefore compelled to insist that the coming restoration is in spite of the exiles, not because of their merits; they had been driven from their land because of their sins, and the same sins they had shown in the lands of their exile (vv. 16–21). He repeats the thought in vv. 22f., 31f.

It needs no proof that the centre of this prophecy, vv. 24–28, is based on and is an expansion of the great promise of the New Covenant in Jer. 31: 31–34. For the modern man it seems strange that although the prophets repeatedly betray a knowledge of the words of their predecessors and contemporaries and sometimes carry their message further, yet they never suggest this nor mention them by name—the non-mention of Jeremiah by Ezekiel is particularly striking. We must not assume that they were indifferent to plagiarism; it is expressly condemned by Jeremiah (23: 30). It is rather that they were so conscious of being Jehovah's spokesmen that they were not sufficiently concerned with the sundry ways and divers manners by which Jehovah had spoken before them to underscore and stress them. That would have been to stress the means by which the message had come, when the message was what really mattered.

It is doubtful whether Ezekiel really tells us more than Jeremiah. The latter concentrates on the spiritual work, the former, consistently with his whole outlook, sees it as the gracious action of God in all its details. That is perhaps why it is Jeremiah rather than Ezekiel who is quoted in the New Testament in *Hebrews*, in which we see the ritual passing away.

It is doubtful whether Ezekiel wishes to convey any clear-cut idea by clean water (v. 25); to equate it with baptism is to forget that this is a mere symbol also. In v. 25 he is thinking of defilement rather than of guilt and so he uses the picture not of the sacrifices but of the ceremonial cleansings in the Levitical law. He knows that there both blood and water only function through the grace of God. He had not, like Isaiah, been given the vision of the Servant of Jehovah, from whose side should flow both blood and water, and so he is looking through the symbols of the Law to the grace behind them.

Already in 11: 19 we had the promise of the changed heart (cf. p. 48). It is far from easy to translate Hebrew psychology into that of the modern man in the street, for where the latter tends to divide and separate, the Hebrew always thought primarily of man in his wholeness. Probably the best translation here is "will," provided we do not think of it as some independent entity in man. For the Hebrew the heart is the

will as the expression of his complete character.   His heart is
a heart of stone because all parts of his being have been in
revolt against God, so his will could not respond to His voice.
The consequence was that Israel was made incapable of re-
sponding to God, except in part (Isa. 6: 9f.; John 12:39; Rom.
11: 25)—it is hardly necessary to add that this is true of all
men (Rom. 9: 15f.), except as the grace of God is in operation.
For linguistic reasons beyond the scope of this study flesh in
the Old Testament does not have the connotations it has in the
New.[1]   Here, since a heart of stone is something contrary to
nature, a heart of flesh is a natural heart, a will as God designed
it to be.

Spirit (*ruach*), when spoken of as part of a man, again does not
bear the meaning generally given it, but tends to mean his
dominant disposition, even an overmastering inclination.[2]
Here, obviously the new spirit is God's spirit, which is to become the dominating factor in transformed Israel.   Hence there
will be the desire and urge to do God's will.

THE NATIONAL RESURRECTION OF ISRAEL (37: 1–14)

The long sweep of Israel's history from Sinai to the Babylonian exile is the process by which God taught men in general
and Israel in particular that national election and blood descent
were inadequate for the creation of a people for God's own
possession, a kingdom of priests and a holy nation.   This goal
could only become a fulfilled reality, when all its members had
passed through the transforming experience that made of Jacob
an Israel.   Until then "they are not all Israel that are of
Israel."

Ezekiel has already given us the picture of God's king, of the
transformed land and people.   He now turns and examines the
coming into being of this revived people of God.   At the beginning of it all in order to stress that the blessing that should
come in and through Abraham was the gift of God's grace and
not the fruit of man's merit, God continued the line of promise
by the "miracle child" Isaac.   Now to stress that the coming
transformation is purely of the grace of God and not in some
way the fruit of the merit of the Fathers, Ezekiel has a strange
trance-vision.

There is no suggestion that the dry bones in the valley are
Israelite bones.   The second half of v. 11 precludes the first
half from being understood in any other sense than that the

---

[1] There is an interesting discussion in J. A. T. Robinson: *The Body.*

[2] See especially Snaith: *The Distinctive Ideas of the Old Testament*, ch. vii.

bones *represent* "the whole house of Israel." Ezekiel sees in reality or in vision—who will dogmatize where he is concerned?—the skeletons of an army ambushed and overwhelmed ("these slain," v. 9) in the desert. Just as John the Baptist had to say that God could raise up from the stones around him children unto Abraham, so the new Israel, though Israel, yet in one sense would have no living link with the past; it would be God's miraculous creation.

Is the Church Israel?

We must pause, however, for a few minutes to consider a question which may have been growing in the minds of some readers. Is not Ezekiel in fact prophesying of the Church in these chapters? Is not the Church the New Israel, and so far as the Jew is envisaged at all, are not these promises fulfilled spiritually for him, when he is converted and becomes a member of the Church?

That the Church is the new people of God is beyond question. Equally certain is that the old people is a prefiguring of it; we need look no further than I Pet. 2: 9 for proof, where the Old Testament titles of Israel are applied to the Church. In passing it is worth saying, that it is only the failure to realize to what extent the New Testament Church has taken to itself all the titles and honours of Israel—for a most striking example see I Cor. 10: 1—that has led to the widespread superstition that certain parts of the New Testament, e.g. Hebrews, James, I Peter, were written exclusively to Jewish Christians. But for all that the title Israel is never applied to the Church. Rom. 11: 26 *in its context* should be quite clear for the Pauline usage and prevent us interpreting Gal. 6: 16, "the Israel of God," in a non-natural way of the Church. When we find the Church constantly being called Israel in the sub-apostolic period, without the least doubt as to the rightfulness of the usage, we should respect the refusal of the New Testament writers to do the apparently obvious.

It is beyond cavil or question that what the Lord promises Israel, 36: 24–27; Jer. 31: 31–34, is what He has done to us in Jesus Christ. The fulfilment for Israel can neither be greater nor less nor other than for us. Yet it is noteworthy that the former passage is not quoted in the New Testament, and though the latter lies behind Mark 14: 24 and parallels, and is quoted in Heb. 8: 8–12 and 10: 16f., it is given in terms of description rather than fulfilment, by which I mean that there is no suggestion that the promise has been exhausted in the Church's enjoyment of it.

We do not question the assertion that promises made under the old covenant have been lifted to a new level in their fulfilment in the new. This perforce means that the language of the promise must as often as not be regarded as symbolic rather than literal. But it is one thing to recognize the symbolic nature of so much prophetic promise, it is quite another to *spiritualize* it to mean something quite other than it could possibly have meant to the original hearers. The transference of symbolic images is harder than many think, hence the grossly materialistic nature of much modern prophetic interpretation, but the spiritualization of Scripture is seldom a spiritual process. It is normally the substitution of the expositor's own views for the teaching of Scripture.

Unless he can give full weight both to the transformed land of Israel in ch. 36 and to the national resurrection of Israel in ch. 37, the expositor has no right to banish the Israel of the old covenant from the picture in favour of the Church. On the other hand we are under no obligation to distort the whole balance of this book by entering into a discussion of the most difficult problem of the relation of the old people of God to the new, of the saved "all Israel" (Rom. 11: 26) to the bride of Christ (but see p. 143).

THE PROPHECY TODAY

Few of the details of the prophecy call for closer attention. We should, however, note that in vv. 5, 6, 8, 9, 10, 14 we have in the English translations the alternation of breath, wind and spirit, when there is only the one word (*ruach*) in the Hebrew. It is questionable whether it is possible to do justice to the Hebrew in English. Note that "the four winds" (v. 9) means the four quarters of the earth.

Our interpretation must depend in some measure on our translation of v. 7. RSV and Moffatt render "rattling," Knox "stirring," but such translations, though theoretically possible, seem out of place. RV seems justified in translating "earthquake"—the meaning of AV "shaking," cf. 38: 19f. Not only is *ra'ash* the technical word for earthquake, but in passages where it is otherwise translated it is clear enough that the trembling of the ground is intended, whether literal or metaphorical, viz. 3: 12 (RV "rushing"); Isa. 9: 5 (RV "tumult"); Jer. 10: 22 (RV "commotion"); 47: 3 (RV "rushing"); Nah. 3: 2 (RV "rattling"); Job 39: 24 (RV "fierceness"). In the only two cases where the earthquake does not come directly into the picture, viz. 12: 18 (RV "trembling") and Job 41: 29

(AV "shaking," RV "rushing"), it seems clear enough that the type of shaking caused by an earthquake is intended.

The coming of the bones together is not by their own action but by the earthquake shaking that follows on the prophetic word. Only then does the miracle of growth begin.

The bones *were very dry*. The return from exile was no true restoration of national life. It is more a religious community than a national state that we meet in *Ezra* and *Nehemiah*. There was no time, not even under the shortlived Hashmonean rule (140–63 B.C.), when anything like a majority of Jews was living in Palestine. It was no accident that the people turned to Simon, a priest, and elected him as "leader and high priest for ever, until there should arise a faithful prophet and . . . captain over them" (I Macc. 14: 41f.), instead of turning to the senior living descendant of the house of David. The pattern set then became even more obvious after the destruction of the second temple, when we find that rule in scattered Jewry is almost entirely in the hand of the rabbis. Though the existence of the Jews was always hard and bitter, a new and even more dreadful chapter began in 1879 with the rise of modern anti-semitism in Germany; it spread rapidly to Russia and then right round the world. Just in this period traditional ortho-doxy was crumbling rapidly, and so Jewry was shaken to the core as perhaps it had not been since the destruction of the first temple. But it was in this shaking that suddenly a new national consciousness sprang to birth. In just over fifty years from the first Zionist conference an independent Jewish state existed for the first time since 63 B.C. All it needs is the Spirit of God.

Notice the skill used in describing God's work in vv. 12–14 resting on the ambiguity of *ruach*. Though God's breath or spirit must be upon them so that they may return to their land (v. 14), yet the giving of true spiritual life follows on the return to the land (v. 12f.). This is also the order in ch. 36: 24–28.

The earthquake shock has passed over Israel; in part he has returned to his land in a consciously national sense, though there are still at least five times as many outside the land than in it. How long it will be before the spiritual transformation takes place is hidden in the councils of God, but we have every reason for believing that it is not far off.

ONE PEOPLE, ONE KING, ONE GOD (37: 15–28)

Already in v. 11 Ezekiel had spoken of "the whole house of Israel"; now he makes it clear that he was using the term in its

full sense.   He is speaking not merely of those loyal families
from the North who had joined Judah from time to time—v. 16,
"Judah and the Israelites attached to him" (Moffatt), cf. II
Chron. 11: 13, 16; 15: 9—but also of those who had survived
from the fall of the Northern Kingdom—"Joseph and all in
Israel attached to him" (Moffatt).   To my way of thinking this
is one of those passages which demolish a popular answer to the
British-Israel theory, viz. that the Jew does in fact represent
all the tribes.   Equally I am incapable of understanding how
the British-Israelite theory can be reconciled with the general
picture in this chapter, for all parts of Israel are equally com-
prehended in the dry bones.   Yet again it is hard to see how
the most hardened allegorizer and spiritualizer can find the
Church here.   Nor can the small companies of "Israel" who
doubtless joined Judah at the return from exile be considered
in any sense a fulfilment.

An adequate discussion of the problem would have to include
a consideration of a number of other Old Testament passages,
notably *Hosea* and parts of Jer. 30, 31, and it would be quite
out of keeping with the scale of this present study.   There seem
to be only three answers to the problem.

The British-Israel answer, quite apart from what seem to
me insuperable difficulties in its Biblical exegesis and general
arguments, just does not fit into the general picture of this
chapter.   There is no question of a powerful company of nations
united to a nationally resurrected Judah, but both Judah and
Israel have been resurrected together.

The view that what is left of the Northern Tribes is scattered
through the mountains of the Middle East[1] may very well be
true.   It has, however, the same doubtful merit of certain
"futurist" interpretations of prophecy; there seems to be no
means whatsoever of establishing the truth or error of the view
until the time of fulfilment comes.

We should, however, seriously consider another possibility.
In pp. 102ff. we considered the problem of "unfulfilled" prophecy and saw that "all national prophecy is conditional."   Seeing
that the statement in Jer. 18: 7–10 comes in a context of God's
dealings with Judah and Jerusalem (Jer. 18: 11), the principle
that prophecy is conditional must be applied to Israel as well
as to the nations.   The never-dying hatred towards the Jew by
the Samaritans, predominantly Israelite in spite of mixed blood
and by their own claim the legitimate descendants of Ephraim,
suggests their obstinate refusal to accept God's verdict in his-

---

[1] Cf. J. Wilkinson: *Israel My Glory*, pp. 103–109.

tory, and it may well have been the attitude of the majority of those that found themselves in exile as well. Such an attitude persisted in through centuries may well have excluded them from God's gracious purposes. Sufficient of the Northern Tribes joined Judah under the divided monarchy and doubtless at the return from exile to make the modern Jew representative of "all Israel" (Rom. 11: 26), and it may be that Ezek. 37: 15–22 will never have a literal fulfilment. God's honour is bound to the ultimate salvation of "all Israel," but this does not imply that any section of the children of Israel must of necessity come within this salvation, for "they are not all Israel, which are of Israel" (Rom. 9: 6). So it may be that the gracious promises to the Northern Tribes of restoration will only have their fulfilment in the descendants of them that clave to Judah.

The climax and purpose of transformed land and people under the king of God's choosing (37: 24f.) is that God's sanctuary should be among them for ever. The implications of this will be considered later, when we deal with ch. 40–48, but it is clear that Ezekiel is foreseeing the fulfilment of prophecies like Isa. 2: 2–4; Mic. 4: 1–4 and many others.

THE FINAL REVOLT (CH. 38, 39)

Before we begin to try to understand these chapters we should ask ourselves at what point in the process described in ch. 34–37 we are to place them. Though there is no intrinsic objection to the suggestion that Ezekiel is looking back to a time earlier than the time when the Lord's "sanctuary shall be in the midst of them for evermore," yet both the actual position of the chapters and 38: 8, 11f., 14, suggest that they belong after the events described in ch. 36, 37. This is confirmed by Rev. 20: 7–10, which is post-millennial. If we are sincere in our affirmation of the authority of Scripture, then we must bow to the interpretation that Scripture sets on itself, instead of insisting on our own. There are but two mentions of Gog in Scripture, here and in *Revelation*, and unless we can produce very cogent arguments to the contrary, we must let the latter interpret the former.[1] To place Gog before the Second Advent and then to add "but includes also the final revolt of the nations at the close of the kingdom-age," as does the Scofield Bible (p. 883),

---

[1] It is worth noting that both in apocalyptic literature, e.g. Enoch 56, 2 Esdras 13, and in earlier Rabbinic writings the usual dating of Gog is in or after the Messianic period. For the Rabbinic evidence see Strack and Billerbeck: *Kommentar zum Neuen Testament aus Talmud und Midrasch*, Vol. III, p. 832ff., Klausner: *The Messianic Idea in Israel*, pp. 496–501.

seems an illegitimate attempt to have the best of it both ways. The only real basis for the common view that these chapters see their fulfilment before the Second Advent is in 39: 21–29[1] It is, however, far more satisfactory to look on these verses as a summary of the message of this whole section of *Ezekiel*.

If we place Gog at the end of the Millennium, we will not concern ourselves very much with the identification of the names mentioned. The curious are referred to *New Bible Commentary, ad loc.*, or to G. H. Lang (*op. cit.*). The statement in the Scofield Bible (p. 883), "That the primary reference is to the northern (European) powers, headed up by Russia, all agree," is an excellent example of the wish being father to the thought. Quite apart from the many who have always refused to identify Rosh with Russia, there is a strong tendency among moderns, e.g. RSV, Knox, Bertholet, ICC, to return to the old Hebrew Massoretic tradition and to translate with AV and RV mg. "chief prince." If we want to identify Meshesh and Tubal, it should surely be as in 27: 13, though 32: 26 (see p. 116) suggests the real meaning (see below).

There is, however, another element we should take into consideration. These chapters are neither predominantly symbolic (at least obviously so) nor minutely descriptive. They are typical of so many descriptions of the future, where the general purpose seems clear enough but the detail is blurred, when we examine it more closely, or is far more general in character than we realize at first reading. Though it would be wrong on these grounds to take for granted that the names are not to be understood literally, yet all analogy points in that direction. When we find that all the names are of tribes on the fringe of the then known world: north, Gog, Magog, Meshesh, Tubal, Gomer, Beth-Togarmah; east, Persia (only just beginning to make its appearance on the Iranian plateau); south, Cush and Put, it becomes intrinsically most probable that we are dealing with a symbolic use, and Rev. 20: 8 confirms this by calling them "the nations which are in the four corners of the earth."

How then are we to understand the whole prophecy in the light of its New Testament placing? If we accept the conception of a Millennium, of God's rule on earth, when Satan is bound, the curse lifted and saved Israel a centre of blessing on

[1] For a careful exposition of this view, which tries to do justice to various divergent opinions, see G. H. Lang: *The Histories and Prophecies of Daniel*, Appendix C (2nd edit.). That careful thinker, E. Sauer, both in his *The Triumph of the Crucified* and his *From Eternity to Eternity* places Gog at the end of the Millennium.

the earth, what room is there for any such outburst of revolt
against God?

There are two ways in which we can look at the world and
man's history on it, from man's position and from God's.
From the former man seems to be an end in himself, and his
history a story of a long, slow climb with many a slip back
from the animal and primitive barbarity until in an age yet
future he reaches perfection.   Such a view can be and often is
held together with a thoroughly Scriptural view of sin, of the
Incarnation and of the Atonement, with the history of revelation regarded primarily as a history of man's salvation.   Much
could be quoted from the Scriptures to support such a view.
From the latter standpoint the creation and history of man are
placed within a wider framework of a Divine purpose.   We are
given little more than hints about this framework—perhaps to
discourage idle speculation, perhaps because we could not
understand, if we were told more—but, alas, the less we are
told the more some profess to know.

Within this framework we see God vindicating His character
and purposes before principalities and powers in heavenly
places.   The salvation of man is not an end in itself, but a
means to a higher end.   Behind all the changes and chances of
human life stands the sovereign love of God, too great and too
high for the mind of man to comprehend in its fullness.   We see
salvation available to all, for the shadow of the cross stretches
from the creation of the world to its end, and He who died on
it is the Light that lighteneth every man.   In every age the
question has been whether man will re-enact Adam's sin, speaking himself free of his Creator, or whether he will turn to Him
in penitence praying "God be merciful to me a sinner."

Scripture shows us that in all ages, with all their varying circumstances of ignorance or knowledge, man has set his will
against God and has failed.   The bulk of the Old Testament
teaches the failure of the children of Israel, and that is after all
the gravamen of Ezekiel's message, see especially chs. 16, 20, 23.
The New Testament introduces us to the beginnings of trouble
in the Church, and makes it clear that they will grow worse
rather than better.   Here too, in the mysterious purpose of
God, alongside His triumphs in the individual is set the failure
of the organization.

The final proof of the failure of man is to be his response,
when placed in the most favourable position conceivable.
Though the sanctuary of God is with man, though the curse
is lifted from nature, though the tempter, the enemy of God
and man is bound, yet when the opportunity is offered, the

deep-seated rebellion in the hearts of so many at once becomes
obvious.   I do not know whether we are to understand the
names symbolically as of those who have kept far from the
glory of God centred in Jerusalem, or whether it refers above
all to those who in previous dispensations had not been exposed
so directly to God's testing.   In either case there is no contradiction between 38: 4, where God is pictured as drawing Gog
to his doom, and Rev. 20: 8, where Satan is portrayed as the
deceiver of the nations.   Man must be put to the test, or else
it will not be clear what is in him.   Satan is the willing instrument by which the testing is carried out.

CHAPTER XIV

THE LORD IS THERE

PROBLEMS OF INTERPRETATION (CH. 40–48)

OUR main difficulty in approaching ch. 40–48 is that the average reader, whether or not they are well known to him, assumes that he already knows the general line of interpretation to be adopted. "Of course," says one, "these are Ezekiel's plans for the worship of the post-exilic community." "No," says another, "obviously we have the plans for the Millennial Temple." "But stay," says another, "quite definitely . . ."

When we add to all this the fact that the upholders of one view will equate the holding of it with scholarship, and the upholders of another with orthodoxy, the task of the expositor becomes peculiarly difficult. To deal with the subject adequately would need a book in itself. I have made two assumptions. In taking for granted that these chapters are genuine revelation, I have ruled out all interpretations which regard the vision form as a mere literary convention or the trance confirmation of theories already formed. In applying II Tim. 3:16 to all Old Testament Scriptures and in regarding the Revelation of John as authoritative in the interpretation of Old Testament symbolism I have virtually ruled out any purely literal interpretation. The interpretation I offer is no *a priori* one forced on Ezekiel, but it has forced itself on me as a result of my reading of the prophecy.

We must free ourselves from the assumption made by so many that we may read from 39:29 to 40:1 without a break. Our study of the book should have showed us that, except in the prophecies against the nations, the dates marked, as it were, new chapters in the development of Ezekiel's message. Surely that must be the case here, for, to us at least, the date has no discoverable historical significance.

Josephus (*Ant.* X, v. 1) says, "Ezekiel . . . left behind him in writing two books concerning these events." Quite apart from the fact that we know of no apocryphal or pseudepigraphic book of Ezekiel, he is obviously referring to canonical Scripture. He can only mean that in his time (first cent. A.D.) part of Ezekiel circulated separately, or that the prophecy was regarded as

consisting of two books. Young suggests that the second book
was ch. 33–48,[1] but to me this is most unlikely. Ch. 33–39
need ch. 1–32 for their understanding and are in turn necessary
to balance the opening chapters. In addition 39: 25–29 would
make a fitting conclusion to the first book, which ch. 32 would
not.

Above all ch. 40–48 are in large part not prophecy, in the
normal biblical sense, but "apocalyptic." For much of the
time Ezekiel is no longer the hearer and assimilator of God's
message, but the mere transmitter of a vision explained by an
angel guide. We shall examine the reason for this later, but
for the moment it is sufficient to note that these chapters seem
to be an independent entity, dependent in some measure on the
earlier prophecies but not necessarily directly continuing them.

The Prophecy is Millennial

We should take the fact seriously that the prophecy is millennial (see p. 12). The temple, and presumably the city, are on
top of a very high mountain (40: 2; 43: 12). This links at once
with prophecies like Isa. 2: 2–4; Mic. 4: 1–4; Zech. 14: 10.
Though there are those that take this literally, I feel convinced
that this is only due to ignorance of the Oriental thought of the
Bible. The meaning of the symbol is suggested by Dan. 2: 34f.,
44f., and it is ultimately derived from the age-old belief that
the gods lived on inaccessible mountain peaks.

But if the vision is millennial, we ought seriously to ask ourselves why it was given to Ezekiel. Can we really say, "It
need hardly be said that Ezekiel has here advanced plans which
he expected to be carried out to the letter"?[2] Prophet after
prophet has given us pictures of what is to follow the Day of
the LORD, and one and all are driven to metaphor and symbol.
Are we seriously to believe that Ezekiel alone among them is
to be taken quite literally, and that he lays down the plans and
rules of the new temple just to save the generation of its builders
the task of discovering the Divine will? Or are we even to
believe, as some seem to do, that there is spiritual gain in recon-
structing in plan and model what Ezekiel saw? Already on
p. 108 I pointed out the danger of ignoring Jewish exposition.
So far from taking these chapters literally of the distant future
the rabbis found themselves under compulsion to explain away
the differences between them and the Law. We are told that
Rabbi Hananiah ben Hezekiah (first cent. A.D.) bought 300

[1] *An Introduction to the Old Testament*, p. 234.

[2] NBC, p. 663b.

measures of oil for his lamp, but before they were used up he
was able to explain the deviations and so rehabilitate the book.
In this connexion it is of importance to note that the rabbis
seem to have believed that sacrifice would cease in the Messianic
age.[1]

The answer is surely given by the New Testament counterpart, John's vision of the New Jerusalem (Rev. 21). There
have been those so devoid of understanding of the symbolic,
that the figures of Rev. 21: 16f. have merely acted as a challenge to them for mathematical and architectural calculation.
Surely they are but part of the wonder and the glory of the
vision which draws the heart of the Christian with longing:

> Jerusalem the golden
>   With milk and honey blest
> Beneath thy contemplation
>   Sink heart and voice opprest . . .
> For thee, O dear, dear country
>   Mine eyes their vigils keep:
> For very love, beholding
>   Thy happy name, they weep.

Or as Bunyan says with such touching brevity, when he has
seen Christian and Hopeful safely into the Celestial City, "I
wished myself among them."

Should we put Ezekiel's vision on a lower level for him and
his friends? Our anti-sacerdotalism and unfamiliarity with
anything that could suggest the temple and its worship render
us probably incapable of understanding the spiritual satisfaction of the exiled priest as he sees the ideal temple ideally served.

THE PROPHECY IS SYMBOLIC

We should also ask ourselves whether the vision is meant to
be taken literally at all. There must be very many who will
hesitate to demand this of "the very high mountain" (40: 2),
or of an absolutely square city about $1\frac{1}{4}$ mile each way (48: 16)
—incidentally the literalist may like to explain why the future
world capital is so small—or of tribal portions divided by dead
straight lines running east and west and ignoring all the facts
of geography (48: 1–29), for the boundaries of the prairie states
in America are hardly a good analogy.

But what are we to say of the river in 47: 1–12? At the
very top of the highest peak the waters issue out in the sanctuary (v. 1). After flowing across the court it trickles (v. 2,

[1] Montefiore and Loewe: *A Rabbinic Anthology*, p. 669.

RV mg., ICC) under the eastern gate. A little more than a quarter of a mile eastwards the waters have become a stream ankle-deep (v. 3). In the next half-mile or so it deepens first to the knees and then to the waist (v. 4). Little more than another quarter of a mile suffices to make it a deep river which can only be crossed by swimming (v. 5). Unless we are to assume a unique and gratuitous miracle, this is a river such as the human eye has never seen nor will ever see. I grant that a friend, whose knowledge of Scripture and wise judgment I deeply respect, once wrote saying, "Have you never heard of tributaries?" But that is to overlook that the river is water of life, water from the Sanctuary of God; there can be no adding of common water.

To me it seems indubitable that the river of Ezek. 47 is the river of Rev. 22: 1f. Ezekiel saw the throne of God against the background of the Babylonian plain (1: 3) and of an earthly temple (8: 4); John saw it in heaven (Rev. 4: 2), but it was the same throne. Even so Ezekiel saw the river of water of life against the background of the parched and thirsty Wilderness of Judea, while John saw it in the new earth, but it is the same river, a river which already flows (cf. John 7: 37f.), for the believer's body is a sanctuary of the Holy Ghost (I Cor. 6: 19, RV mg.).

For me the fact that both the setting of the vision and one of its most important parts are symbolic is sufficient to show that the whole is to be taken as symbolic. There are few so prosaic that they will object to the use of metaphor and simile in a matter-of-fact description. But we are much slower to realize that one who is dealing in avowed symbolism is capable of using the most concrete descriptions in a symbolic sense. The bread and wine set out on the Lord's Table are capable of description in the exactest physical terms, but even the believer in Transubstantiation will hasten to say that these are accidents and that the true use of the elements is symbolic.

ANIMAL SACRIFICE

For those that take this section seriously as a Divine revelation and not merely as Ezekiel's programme for the future clothed in vision form, the sacrifices provide the real crux in its interpretation. Make the sacrifices symbolic and the temple becomes symbolic too; take the temple literally and we have to agree that there will be animal sacrifices in the Millennium. I have no difficulty in a vision of sacrifice in a symbolic temple, for it was the guarantee to Ezekiel that the great principles of

Divine redemption remained good to the end of time, but I require stronger evidence than this vision to accept against all the weight of New Testament evidence that the Levitical sacrifices will be reintroduced.

The paradox of *Hebrews*, "Apart from shedding of blood there is no remission" (9: 22), and "It is impossible that the blood of bulls and goats should take away sins" (10: 4) is already latent in the Old Testament.   Already in Num. 15: 30f. we have a major limitation on the efficacy of animal sacrifices, for they are there declared unavailing for deliberate sin; there is, however, nowhere in the Old Testament any suggestion that those who commit deliberate sin are finally cut off from Divine forgiveness.   Whether it be in the cry of Psa. 51: 1–17, with its express disclaimer of sacrifice in v. 16, or in the reiterated prophetic appeal to repentance (cf. especially Ezek. 18), there is the clear vision of Jehovah, "a God merciful and gracious, slow to anger, and abounding in steadfast love and faithfulness keeping steadfast love for thousands, forgiving iniquity and transgression and sin . . ." (Ex. 34: 6f., RSV), which is basic to the whole Old Testament revelation.   The sacrifices stand as a perpetual mysterious reminder that forgiveness is dependent on more than God's grace, but this something does not begin to be truly revealed until Isa. 52: 13 – 53: 12.

Ezekiel's vision underlines the promise of Jer. 3: 16f., for there is no ark and mercy seat in the new temple.   Why should we think that Ezekiel failed to rise to the level of his prophetic predecessors, who, though they did not reject sacrifices, as an earlier generation of scholars thought, yet relegated them to a purely secondary place of no real or vital importance?   Indeed, one of the most remarkable features of this book is its virtual ignoring of sacrifices until this section, and even here there is relatively little said about them.   The explanation given above as to why they are mentioned at all is surely sufficient.

Presumably all who regard the temple as millennial and take the sacrifices literally would subscribe to the statement in the Scofield Bible (p. 890): "Doubtless these offerings will be memorials, looking back to the cross, as the offerings under the old covenant were anticipatory, looking forward to the cross. In neither case have animal sacrifices power to put away sin (Heb. 10: 4; Rom. 3: 25)."[1]   Though I fully recognize their sincerity, I must beg them to realize that those who cannot follow with them are no despisers of the Scriptures.   They read *Hebrews* to mean that the abolition of the Aaronic priesthood

---

[1] For a strong defence of this view see Sauer: *From Eternity to Eternity*, Ch. XXXIV.

and of the Levitical sacrifices is final and for ever. In addition they cannot see why, when water, bread and wine have met the symbolic needs of nearly a thousand generations of Christians, the Millennium will need more. The King has returned and the curse on nature has been lifted; why should the animal creation still lay down its life?

The fact is that the ultra-dispensationalist is apt so to divide up the revelation of God that he fails to see it in its completeness. Above all he fails to realize that while human response to the Divine revelation may ebb and flow, the revelation itself never turns back but always deepens. There is presumably more privilege in this dispensation for the predestinated member of the Church, but in the Millennium, as the temporal prepares itself for the eternal, there will be neither less knowledge nor blessing. Indeed I find it hard to believe that it is meant seriously, when I am told that our present freedom for all to worship equally in all places will be replaced by a position in which man's privilege of worship will depend in measure on his geographical relationship to an earthly Jerusalem. The suggestions of supersonic aircraft bringing pilgrims to Jerusalem and of others sharing in the temple services by television are tragi-comic.

Present or Future?

Those who see in these chapters above all blue-prints for the post-exilic community point to passages like 43: 7f.; 44: 6–16 and ask whether they can possibly refer to any other time than the prophet's own and that of the return from exile. They are quite right. The vision of the perfect temple led to a rebuke of the failings of the past. But this is precisely paralleled by Rev. 21:1–22:15. Here too the basis is a vision with an angel guide; here too the voice of God breaks through the vision from time to time, and here too are passages, e.g. 21: 6ff., 27; 22: 6f., 11–15, whose chief applicability is to this present age. A vision of the future that does not change the present has failed in its main purpose.

Expositors have signally failed to agree whether in Rev. 21f. we have a vision of the eternal state, of the Millennium, or even of the Church here and now (that the New Jerusalem is the Church is clear from Rev. 21: 9f.). But we should not be surprised at this. The Millennium is the antechamber of and the preparation for the eternal state. Its glories are less than those of eternity, but they are of the same nature. Even now the Church is with its Lord in the heavenlies, and those whom God has called He has already glorified (Rom. 8: 29f.), at least in His sight.

Equally it would be unwise to tie down Ezekiel's vision in time. He sees the generation of the Return, "the holy seed" (Ezr. 9: 2), not as man sees them, but as they were in God's purpose. More obviously it is Israel, when the promise of the new covenant, of the new heart and new spirit is fulfilled. They are symbolized by the small but perfect temple. Since they are "a kingdom of priests and an holy nation" (Ex. 19: 6), the secular power is symbolized by the prince (*nasi'*)—he will not call him king, lest the rule of God be obscured—who is seen only in a secondary role. For the literalist the identity of the prince must be a major problem, for he cannot be the King who has returned, Jesus the Messiah.

But I believe Ezekiel saw further. The city has had only casual mention (45: 6, 48: 15), but at the close of the vision it suddenly fills the eye, and it is of the city that the closing words are spoken, "the LORD is there." The Shekinah glory has moved from temple to city (cf. Jer. 3: 17), and if so, where is the need of a temple any longer? So in Rev. 21 the temple has vanished and we see only the city. But since it is no longer the restored remnant of Israel, but the Church from every nation and tongue and kindred, in which the old and the new are united—the gates bear the names of the twelve tribes of Israel (Rev. 21: 12; Ezek. 48: 31–34) and the foundations the names of the apostles of the Lamb (Rev. 21: 14)—the city has increased from a square of 1¼ miles a side to one of 1,500 miles a side (Rev. 21: 16). Further it has become the mountain itself, for it is as high as it is broad. Many speak of the New Jerusalem as a cube and think of the Holy of Holies. They forget that though this may serve as a verbal symbol, it will hardly make sense as a visual one. The New Jerusalem is the mountain of God that fills the earth.

In Rev. 4 we find the imagery of the *merkabah* from Ezek. 1 taken up and expanded on a more glorious scale. Even so Ezek. 40–48 is taken up and expanded in Rev. 21, 22, and "the LORD is there" finds its fulfilment in, "I saw no temple therein: for the Lord God the Almighty and the Lamb, are the temple thereof." Here too is the explanation of why Ezekiel passed from normal prophecy to apocalyptic. Again and again as we have read his prophecies we have faced the element of the contingent, but here we deal with the certainties of the Divine purpose. "The zeal of the LORD of hosts shall perform this." The City of God, the Church of the Living God, is foreknown and predestinated before the foundation of the world. There can be no peradventure and no improvization in God's victory and the fulfilment of His purpose.   Hence Ezekiel, like John after him, sees the vision of what already is in the mind and purpose of God.   The measurements, though they have their elements of fairly transparent symbolism, serve above all to stress that the final structure has conformed in all points to the architect's will and purpose.   The day is surely coming, when all shall see that God's purpose with Israel, with the Church and with the nations has been altogether perfect and successful.